The Art of Conflict-Free Negotiations

6 Steps to Winning Without Conflict. How to Analyze People and Understand Their True Intentions, Dreams, and Desires.

HALBERT WARD

© Copyright 2024 - All rights reserved.

The content inside this book may not be duplicated, reproduced, or transmitted without direct written permission from the author or publisher.

Under no circumstances will any blame or legal responsibility be held against the publisher, or author, for any damages, reparation, or monetary loss due to the information contained within this book, either directly or indirectly.

Legal Notice:

This book is copyright protected. It is only for personal use. You cannot amend, distribute, sell, use, quote or paraphrase any part, or the content within this book, without the consent of the author or publisher.

Disclaimer Notice:

Please note the information contained within this document is for educational and entertainment purposes only. All effort has been executed to present accurate, reliable, up to date, complete information. No warranties of any kind are declared or implied. Readers acknowledge that the author is not engaging in the rendering of legal, financial, medical, or professional advice. The content within this book has been derived from various sources. Please consult a licensed professional before attempting any techniques outlined in this book.

By reading this document, the reader agrees that under no circumstances is the author responsible for any losses, direct or indirect, that are incurred as a result of the use of the information contained within this document, including, but not limited to, errors, omissions, or inaccuracies.

TABLE OF CONTENT

INTRODUCTION	4
CHAPTER ONE	
Solutions that Work	10
CHAPTER TWO	
Dealing with Difficult People	21
CHAPTER THREE	
Conflict Resolution Skills	29
CHAPTER FOUR	
The Resolution Process	36
CHAPTER FIVE	
Successful Negotiations	52
CHAPTER SIX	
The Psychology of Negotiation	66
CHAPTER SEVEN	
Mindset of a Negotiator	75
CHAPTER EIGHT	
Negotiators and Body Language	81
CHAPTER NINE	
Dealing with Emotions in Negotiations	92
CHAPTER TEN	
Attitude in Negotiation	101
CONCLUSION	107

INTRODUCTION

Every individual is always negotiating, and this makes you a negotiator whether you like it or not. Many people arrive at decisions through negotiation, whether in business or family dealings. You discuss with your workers the salary you are willing to pay them and the quality of work you want them to provide in return. When you want to purchase a new piece of machinery, you bargain with the salesman for the price. You negotiate with the client for an acceptable business deal for your company. You also negotiate the terms of your loan with your lender when taking a loan. You cannot separate negotiation from life; it is a part of our everyday life activities.

There are some steps you can take to win without conflict. We discuss those steps in this book. They will teach how to negotiate and win without negativity.

Having negotiation skills is critical for business today. And this is a thing that no one can avoid. Whether it is settling a dispute, overcoming conflict with partners or colleagues, or determining the terms of a new deal, negotiating is part of our everyday personal and professional lives.

Every party taking part in a negotiation has distinct perspectives and interests, and they want to perform well and leave the negotiation table with the best they can get. When you are negotiating with business partners or colleagues who negotiate in a context that is non-integrative or who are particularly competitive, the situation can even become more complicated.

So what can you do to navigate negotiation and ensure that you arrive at the best outcomes, concessions, and agreements for your business and yourself?

This book will help you learn a variety of strategies for effective negotiation.

Top negotiators proactively do some things to achieve better outcomes, and this book will help you learn how to practice those things and become a master at negotiating and win at any negotiation you engage in.

Most people are only aware of two ways to negotiate. The hard or soft way is what they are aware of. The individual who is a hard negotiator views conflict as a battle in which the individual who holds out and stays in the most extreme position performs better. The individual who is a soft negotiator follows the path of peace and makes concessions to resolve conflicts or avoid them. The hard negotiator may destroy or damage the personal relationship they have with the other individual or they may feel that they have exhausted themselves. The soft negotiator may find themselves feeling abused and used. People often feel dissatisfied, hostile, or worn out when they use the typical strategies for negotiation.

Positional bargaining, which is the most popular form of negotiating, depends on giving up positions and successive taking. Think about two individuals haggling over an item's price. Positional bargaining is not necessarily efficient even though it can be successful, and it may not end in a peaceful solution. Negotiators may focus on positions and become more committed to the position than to the original interests or underlying concerns of either party. They may eventually feel that compromise will lead to losing face.

Incentives that stall settlement are also created by positional bargaining. An individual may drag their feet, try to deceive the other individual, take extreme positions, threaten to walk out, stubbornly hold to them, and so on. Rather than working together and trying to come up with a solution that is acceptable, positional bargaining turns into a battle. Any agreement arrived at may reflect splitting of differences, instead of creative and careful development of a solution that is mutually beneficial.

When you negotiate successfully, it can help you when it comes to derailing conflicts, hiring better workers, running a better business, and saving money.

Negotiation involves two or more parties working to achieve a solution that is mutually agreed upon. The solution they are working toward is for a shared issue. You can make deals, build relationships, manage conflicts, and solve problems with your negotiation skills. Although negotiation skills can be learned, some individuals are naturally skilled negotiators.

Negotiation is important when it comes to running a business so it is important that you learn the skills that are necessary to successfully negotiate. As long as you ask in the right way, most things in the world of business are negotiable. You need to know that almost everything is negotiable.

You make many business decisions every day if you are the head of your own company. Some decisions may be small and others may be large. You need to understand that many of these decisions from banking, to inventory, to hiring are negotiable. When you set up the best possible deal from the start, it can save you stress, time, and money down the road. You need strategies for negotiating with an opponent that is intransigent and uncooperative. An individual's uncooperative behavior usually has reasons behind it. Individuals may behave badly in negotiations when they are afraid or angry because they see that the only alternative to being dominated is asserting their own power, because they don't have any idea about any effective way to behave, or because they don't see any benefit from negotiating. The effective negotiator encounters the additional challenge of controlling their own reactions which is an additional challenge for them because intransigent behaviors are likely to cause an angry response.

Controlling one's own behavior is the first step to take when it comes to making the other individual pay attention to you so that you can have an effective negotiation. When faced with a challenging situation, individuals typically either give in, strike back, or break off the relationship. These are responses that are counter-productive. When facing an opponent that is difficult, you can go to the balcony. Instead, of reacting, do not do that. Distance yourself emotionally to keep your mental equilibrium and view the situation objectively. Identify your best alternative to a negotiated agreement and your underlying interests. Decide whether negotiating in the situation is worth it. Take some time to recognize your opponent's tactics, and recognize your own hot-button issues and feelings. When you are negotiating, you can pause, take some time out, or perform a review of the discussion to date so as to gain more time. Don't rush to make a decision. You can withdraw, even if it is for a short period of time, to do a proper review of everything. The next thing to do is step to the opponent's side to disarm them.

After reading this book, lacking what to say during negotiations will be a thing of the past. You will learn to analyze people and read their minds through their body language, and this knowledge will help you negotiate better. An individual may say one thing but actually mean another thing. When you study their nonverbal language in addition to their verbal language, you will gain a full understanding of their desires, dreams, and true intentions.

Body language helps us understand and decode what an individual is saying. We are also able to interpret the emotions and moods of others through body language.

Our conscious understanding of the reactions of individuals to what we say and how we say it is enhanced by body language. It is important to know what makes body language important in communication and how you can improve it. Patience and practice are important when it comes to improving, just as you would do when learning any other skill.

To understand the non-verbal cues, it is important for you to be fully present in the conversation. Otherwise, you will miss the non-verbal cues and not fully understand the conversation.

So, what makes body language important in communication? People do not only hear the words you speak but also your body language. When it comes to your social, personal, and professional success, body language is important. Thus, how the audience interprets your message and receives it will be impacted by your non-verbal cues. If someone is a very good orator, then they should make sure that their body language also matches their personality.

When you know how to use body language and read it correctly, you will find it beneficial in your professional and personal life as it will help you with effective communication.

Body language can be conscious or subconscious and refers to the nonverbal cues you give the person you are talking to. You can gauge how a conversation is going by analyzing other people's body language, and the other party can also get clues about your feelings from your body language. It is an individual's general demeanor during an interaction. People send out different types of physical cues during an interaction, including facial expressions and posture. These nonverbal cues make the other individual understand how we are feeling at a particular time. If you practice effectively, you can master how to use body language to show positive emotions during a conversation and you can also fully understand what the other individual is saying and what they are not saying. When you are having a conversation with someone, holding eye contact with them shows that you are listening to them and you are engaged. If you don't practice consciously, you tend to use habitual body language, and this may not send out the real message that you would want to communicate when you are having a particular interaction.

When you master how to read people's minds and use the skills this book teaches, you will become great at achieving conflict-free negotiations. You may hate negotiations, but this is your chance to turn things around and become great at it. Ready to get started? Read on.

CHAPTER ONE
Solutions that Work

Do you hate engaging in negotiations? Are you worried that you want something different from what the other individual is willing to give? Are you worried about winning, while someone else loses? Well, nobody has to lose; you can still achieve a win-win situation.

It is possible to find a solution that makes all the parties involved winners when you negotiate with a win-win approach. We will discuss win-win negotiation so that you can learn how to use principled negotiation to get the results that you and the other individual who is involved in the negotiation want.

In a win-win negotiation, you explore your own position and that of the other individual to achieve an outcome that is mutually acceptable and gives you and the individual what you want. If you and the other individual walk away with what you got from the deal, you have achieved a win-win negotiation.

In a win-win situation, the other individual wants what you are ready to give, and you are willing to give them what they want. If things are not this way, and one of you must give up what you want for the other individual, then some form of compensation should be negotiated, as this is fair. It is important that both sides feel comfortable with the outcome to achieve a win-win situation.

Ensure that you are flexible and keep an open mind because people may have goals that are different from what you expect. When you want to start a negotiation, a good starting point is to establish a strong position. But conflict can arise and there may be a breakdown in discussion if you get too entrenched.

This can be avoided by using principled negotiation, which is a type of win-win negotiation. You can achieve a successful negotiation when you encourage cooperation toward a common goal.

The following six steps will help you win without conflict:

1. Separate individuals from the situation

You need to first avoid seeing the other individual as your opponent. Ensure that you stay focused on the situation at hand, and try to ignore differences in personality. Emotion, perception, and communication are three factors you need to be aware of.

Perception involves putting yourself in the other person's shoes such that you are in a better position to find a common ground. Although you may believe that your position is right, reasonable, and fair, the other person may also believe the same about their position.

Take time to examine your emotions, acknowledge them, and then ask yourself why you have those feelings. For instance, could your behavior in this negotiation be affected by a previous bad experience you had in a negotiation?

Stay calm as the negotiations go on, as it will help your decision-making process. Study the other person's emotions, and ensure that you do not respond negatively if the conversation becomes heated.

Instead, use your emotional intelligence to find out what made the argument go this way, and do your best to understand the underlying concerns, needs, and interests of each party involved. Ensure that you have precise and clear communication, to avoid having any misunderstandings.

Active listening techniques like listening carefully, looking directly at the person speaking, and allowing the person speaking to finish speaking before you respond are techniques you can use.

2. Stay focused on the individual's interests

Individuals are seldom difficult just because they want to be, and there are valid and real differences sitting behind positions that are conflicting. There are many factors that may influence the way each individual sees the issue. These factors may include their status, beliefs, responsibilities, cultural background, and values.

Avoid blaming anyone and try to have a courteous conversation. Once everybody is sure that their interests have been taken into consideration, they will be more likely to accept different people's points of view.

For instance, if you are having a negotiation with your boss to provide more resources that your team can work with, consider that your boss may be trying to reduce costs and may be under pressure to do this. If you take a closer look beyond your two positions, you may discover that increasing the productivity of your team is a common interest that you have.

Don't focus on positions but on interests. For a solution that is wise and fair, you need to reconcile interests and not positions. Compatible and shared interests as well as interests that are conflicting lie behind opposed positions. A farmer who is trying to purchase a drill needs the drill so that they can get in the wheat crop and then generate income. The dealer of machinery has an investment in the drill and he needs to recover the equipment cost, salaries of salespersons, store overhead costs, interest on borrowed money, and so on. The machinery dealer and the farmer have compatible interests. The machinery dealer wants to sell the drill and the farmer wants to have the drill. Conflicts may start when exchange terms are discussed.

Each party involved in a negotiation has multiple interests. Basic human needs such as economic well-being, security, a sense of belonging, and control over one's life and recognition, are the most powerful interests. Clearly identify all the interests of everyone involved in the negotiation. Ask questions like why, and also ask them why not? Come up with a list of the various interests. You can write them down as you notice them. Be specific and make your interests come alive. When you have concrete details, your interests add impact and they are credible. Avoid implying that the interests of the other side are illegitimate or unimportant.

Acknowledge the other party's interests as part of the issue. If you want your interests to be appreciated by the other side, you can start by showing that you appreciate their interests. Do unto other individuals as you would have those individuals do unto you. If you want an individual to listen to you and completely understand your reasoning, give your reasoning and interests first and then your proposals or conclusions later. Be flexible and concrete. Start your negotiation with interests and options that are well thought out, but ensure that your mind is open.

Be soft on the people and hard on the problem. Look forward and not backward and focus on the problem with your aggressive energy. Two individuals who are negotiating, each pushing hard for their own interests, usually stimulate each other's creativity in creating solutions that are mutually advantageous.

3. Get into the individual's shoes

When you have a good sense of the other individual's desires and you put yourself in their shoes, it will help you to understand their point of view even if you are not in agreement with them. This will make it possible for you to be more present and hopefully facilitate a discussion that is more rational. The other party will know that you are at least listening to them when you are invested in finding out more about them and understanding them. This might result in you being heard and also being better understood. When both individuals who are involved in a negotiation are able to share their perspectives, there is a high likelihood of them feeling equally invested. The right questions can be asked and the right information shared to facilitate the creation of joint value. Listening effectively and understanding where individuals are coming from can help you find potential trade-offs or help you think of issues that you can bring to the table so that you can be able to move the counter-party and the negotiation forward to a mutually beneficial solution.

4. Work towards achieving mutual gain

Each side will most likely understand the other's interests by now, and a solution to the issue at hand might be obvious. You may even be close to concluding an agreement. If this is not the case, remain open to the idea that there may be a completely new position and explore your options by using the negotiation process.

According to our example, if increased productivity is a mutual interest you have identified, but your company is finding it difficult to afford new equipment or staff, you could use this opportunity to assess inexpensive ways, training opportunities, and working practices to increase efficiency.

When looking for a solution to the problem, ensure that you brainstorm as many ideas as possible. Stay open to suggestions, develop the suggestions that are the most promising into proposals, and then present them during negotiation.

5. Make use of objective criteria

This is not just about laying out the facts because different goals, opinions, interests, and underlying needs can make individuals interpret facts differently, or make them go with only those facts that support their position.

For instance, when an interdepartmental negotiation is going on in your company and the discussion is about a new product's launch date, you become convinced that the best option is to rush the product to the market as early as possible. A danger exists that your position could become entrenched, and there could be a lessening of your willingness to listen.

Some evidence supports this view within the marketing data, but also if the launch is delayed until later in the year and it matches with a national holiday, it indicates that it would also be good for sales in the longer term. Your marketing team would also be given more time to prepare a campaign.

Ensure that you agree on a set of criteria that is objective and provide a framework for the discussion you are having. These could include measurements like a mission statement, market value, legal standards, or contractual terms. When you agree on standards, it shows a commitment to reaching an agreement and also demonstrates shared values.

Going back to the example we gave earlier, you and your boss could decide to use a budget as a basis for discussion concerning more resources for your team, and move forward on the basis that any changes must be done within these financial limitations.

6. Know the best alternative that you have to a negotiated agreement

Your best alternative is the fallback option that you want if you are unable to get all that you want. This is different from the bottom line, which is a fixed position that is capable of limiting your options and may stop you from finding a new course of action.

You should think about what might happen if you fail to achieve the result you desire from the negotiation and select the alternatives that you find the most attractive. Pay attention to these alternatives and at the end of everything, the alternative solution that is the most promising is the one you will choose.

Win-Lose Negotiation and Win-Win Negotiation

If you are having a negotiation where you don't need the goodwill of the individual concerned and are not expecting to deal with them again, you may want to use distributive bargaining and seek a bigger piece of the pie for yourself. Distributive bargaining is a win-lose approach often used for negotiating prices for goods or services like a car or house.

Similarly, to gain an advantage, it may be appropriate to push the rules when the stakes are high, but without crossing the line. But, these techniques can have serious drawbacks when you want to have an ongoing relationship that is productive with the individual that you are having a negotiation with.

The drawbacks can include:

Using manipulation and tricks during a negotiation can affect trust and destroy teamwork.

If the person who loses needs to fulfill a part of a deal, the person may become awkward or uncooperative.

If one individual puts the other individual at a disadvantage, there may be reprisals later.

Win-win negotiation can make both parties involved in a discussion feel that the deal they have made is a satisfactory one and that they both won. This is useful when you and the other individual have an ongoing relationship and you wish to maintain a good relationship.

Principled negotiation is a form of win-win strategy that is common. It is capable of helping people negotiate an agreement in a way that is civil.

Winning to get your way feels good. However, winning can become a person's only goal in conflict situations. That is, people can make up their minds to win no matter the costs, which is capable of causing long-term damage.

When people look at conflict as a competition, where one party wins and the other party loses, it becomes hard to collaborate and come up with solutions that provide improved outcomes for all the parties. When we do all we can to win at all costs, what happens is that we are taking another approach that substitutes competition for collaboration. The winning-at-all-costs solution is easy to follow since we live in a fairly competitive society. Certain parts of a competitive attitude can lead to increased performance and outcomes that are better. Yet, we discover especially in conflict settings that trying to win at all costs actually has a cost associated with it.

When individuals feel that other individuals are doing all they can to get their way no matter the costs, they usually get defensive. They usually don't buy into the outcome and they are also not helpful to its implementation. So, the results can be affected by winning at all costs and the relationships can also be jeopardized at the same time. Individuals don't want their interests to be neglected and when a person ignores them because their minds are focused on getting their own way, it can damage relationships. When the relationships are between interdependent people who will need each other's help in the future, this is particularly problematic.

If you are a person who tries hard to get your way and you are highly task-focused, you may want to spend time thinking about whether the behavior you are displaying is a winning-at-all-costs behavior. Slow down and spend time thinking about what you can do to help come up with collaborative solutions that meet the interests you have but that might also handle those of the other individuals in the conflict.

To come up with collaborative solutions, you can listen carefully to the other individual so that you can understand how they see the problem and what their interests may be. You will want to share the perspectives you have and your wants. When it gets to some point, you can start to come up with possible solutions and then check them to see if they address the other individual's interests and meet your needs. When you discover these collaborative solutions that work well for both individuals, getting cooperation in implementing them is easier.

If a win-win is not a compromise, what is it?

Although in a long-term relationship, it may feel appropriate at times for sacrifices to be made by each individual for the relationship's benefit, and the ideal result is not compromise.

A compromise is a settlement of a dispute or agreement that each side making concessions reach. Standards that are not up to what is desirable are then accepted. It can be hard to accept something that is lower than what you have in mind, and compromise involves accepting that.

So, a win-win involves two different sides to the conversation or dispute, and also the desire to resolve the issue. This outcome is different because both parties reach a resolution that everyone agrees to.

Some other outcomes include the win-lose, where you like the outcome but the other individual doesn't because they allowed you to get your way, the lose-win, where the other individual gets what they wanted but you don't get yours because you gave in to them and are unhappy, the lose-lose, where both parties are not happy about the conversation's outcome because they have given up on finding a solution to the issue, and the compromise outcome, where none of the party is particularly satisfied but they are not completely unhappy.

Usually, when there is a conflict, the main issue is that people want different things. This sometimes causes the situation to escalate because there is an ineffective tackling of the differences, which leads to a breakdown in communication, or damage to the relationship's trust. When this has taken place, people usually lose any motivation that they have to solve problems together. They may be where they are not willing to help the other individual. When the two individuals are holding on to this view, moving the issue forward is very hard.

For this reason, mediation is usually used to achieve a win-win outcome. When the mediator is a completely neutral third party, he or she will try to understand the needs of all parties involved. A mediator is usually a specialist in communication, relationships, and conflict, so they are able to understand what is stopping each individual from moving forward.

Before the individuals feel able to solve the problem, they will likely talk about what happened through their perception as they feel the need to be heard, and they will also gain understanding by hearing other people's perceptions. One or two parties may make them understand what they did that worsened the situation.

Very often, when they have a discussion and they get challenged by the mediator after they listen to both parties, one party will see how they have unrealistic expectations or assumptions, and they will understand what is important to them.

Once there are no more obstacles and the individuals get motivated to achieve their desires, they start focusing less on the individual and more on the issue. The mediator then lets each party know what is required to achieve what they want after uncovering what each party really wants.

When a win-win is desired, the aim is to creatively find a solution or some solutions that meet the key aims of each party, and not just to find a solution that is easy and quick. Sometimes, one party might be interested in an action, a word, or a feeling, while at other times, they might be interested in something tangible like money.

What differentiates a win-win from a compromise is that a win-win outcome encourages solutions that are creative and that make both parties involved feel heard and satisfied, while a compromise involves accepting less than what you want and being slightly disappointed.

If you get the right support from a person who is a specialist in conflict issues or if both individuals get the motivation to find a creative solution, achieving a win-win is often very possible.

CHAPTER TWO
Dealing with Difficult People

How can you deal with people who are difficult without causing harm to your mental health?

Dealing with difficult people can be a tough thing to do. An interaction with someone that is really unpleasant can linger in your mind, even when the person is not where you are. When you try to suppress those interactions, your mental health can be affected.

Many times, when you are in a place like a workplace, you might have no choice but to be around these difficult people whether you like it or not. There are some things you can do to reduce the impact these difficult people have on you. Here is how to spot people who are not-so-nice and handle them both in the workplace and out of the workplace.

What makes an individual a difficult person?

Every individual is different. Personality clashes on their own don't result in difficult relationships. What usually ruins interpersonal relationships is criticism, an absence of empathy, and communication problems.

Difficult individuals have these traits:

They are highly critical

It can be challenging to be around individuals who are highly critical as it can seem like nobody or nothing meets their standards. Sadly, their comments sting the more you get closer to them, and this can be very annoying in relationships.

They lack empathy

Some people only care about themselves; they don't care about anyone else. This can make it hard for people to deal with them as they usually find it challenging when it comes to understanding other people's circumstances or emotions. These individuals often come across as uncaring or callous.

They have communication problems

They might never pay attention to what you are saying or constantly speak while you are speaking. They might be rude, passive-aggressive, or indirect. Whatever you are saying to them, it is never easy to have a conversation with them, and you don't feel good after having a conversation with them. Poor communication can negatively affect any relationship.

You would find it much more convenient if difficult people simply walked around letting everyone know about their unpleasantness. But while this doesn't happen, you can see some clear warning signs.

Here are more ways to know someone is a difficult person:

- They insult you or belittle you.
- Other individuals seem to stay away from them.
- They are extremely co-dependent, jealous, or display other red flags in their relationships.
- They insist that everything has to be their own way.
- They always second-guess whatever you do or say.
- They always have an answer to give for everything.
- They display toxic traits, like gossiping, being bossy, or being picky.
- They leave you out when having important conversations.
- They have inconsistent private and public behavior.
- They have problems with emotional regulation.
- You feel uncomfortable around them.

Being around individuals who are difficult can negatively impact workplace culture and your relationships. Because these people's behavior can have a negative impact on your well-being, you need to take steps to stop their behavior from having a negative effect on you. You might say you will not let their negative behavior get to you, but this might be easier said than done.

How can you stop yourself from getting affected by a difficult person?

When you change, others will also change. You need to start working on yourself first so that things can go the way you want them to go. After all, only one person does not get into an argument.

When you know this, you need to first look inside of you whenever you find yourself in a challenging situation with a difficult person. When you understand why you are affected by these individuals, you will be able to determine what to do to manage their behavior well.

In life, we will always meet difficult people at one time or the other. But understanding how their attitudes and behavior affect us can get us ready to deal with them.

So, how do you manage a difficult person?

You can do the following to manage a difficult person better:

Notice your reaction

How does this individual's behavior make you feel? Are you having feelings of frustration, or do you feel dismissed or insulted? If you can label your feelings, you will be able to get out of reactivity mode and into a space that is much more productive.

Do some internal work

Sometimes, we are bothered by some people because they seem to remind us of ourselves. We will not be able to tolerate their shortcomings if we are already feeling frustrated with ourselves or because of the problems we have.

You will find it helpful to work with a coach when it comes to navigating challenging situations. It provides you with the opportunity to depersonalize what is going on and find out if a root conflict that is not related to that individual exists. And if the individual is really being difficult, it's good to have another individual validate that too.

Practice what you want to say

If you are trying to avoid conflict, you may hesitate when it comes to having conversations with difficult people. If this is the case, try practicing whatever it is you wish to say first. You will find coaching sessions helpful when it comes to running through conversations with different personas. You can have the conversation that was intended, talking through different resolutions, or recapping previous exchanges.

Remain calm

It doesn't help to get angry when you are dealing with a difficult person. Staying calm does wonders in this case. Many times, the person will use your justified or unjustified reaction to look for support, making you appear as if you were overreacting.

When you notice that you are getting exasperated with somebody, don't just engage with the person right away. Step back and take a deep breath. You can follow up when your emotions are under control.

Put yourself in their shoes

Once you put yourself in the person's shoes, you can then see things from their point of view. What would justify your behavior if you were this person and you were displaying this behavior? What would you need to see happen to make you believe that you were right? This might help you gain some insight into how the other individual feels.

When you see things from the perspective of the individual, it doesn't mean that you must be in agreement with them. But you will be able to develop compassion for them. This way, you open the way to communicating with respect and compassion.

Listen when they speak

When you find yourself faced with a challenging situation or person, just start by listening and trying to understand what is going on as much as possible. Pay attention to why the person is giving you a hard time and get to know what they actually want. If the person is upset, don't try to shut them down. When you ask them to calm down, it can have the opposite effect especially if the person thinks that you are not really close to them.

Use appropriate humor

Sometimes, we may find ourselves getting into conversations that are difficult because we are not relaxed but take things too seriously. Using appropriate humor when you are in conflict with someone else can help to diffuse tension. You can smile or even crack a joke as it can lower the stakes. It can get you into a more collaborative mood and remind you of shared common ground.

Honor the needs of you and the individual

Many individuals feel that when people look for a middle ground, nobody actually gets what they desire. That is the version of compromise that is the least fulfilling.

Coming to an agreement that meets both of your needs and feels a little more satisfying is what works better. Look for a way to do that with respect. The individual can become a little more pleasant to deal with even if they don't change their ways. Some boundary-setting and mutual understanding can help accomplish that.

Just walk away

If you notice that you are dealing with a person that you find really hard to cope with, you need to get yourself out of there. Sometimes, it is not worth your time, so don't even engage at all. When it has to do with your feelings, you might feel absorbed and forget that you can just leave. It is best to leave so that you don't say or do something you will regret later because it would be much more difficult to unsay or undo anything after you have had some time to reflect.

This is true for people who are difficult. If you are finding it hard dealing with them, just walk away or log off as the case may be. Even if you are standing right in front of them and having a face-to-face conversation, just find a way to leave. You can say you have an important phone call or an emergency to attend to, and then tell them that you will continue the conversation later.

Take care of yourself

It can be emotionally exhausting to be around difficult people even if everything seems to look good on the surface. If you know that you will be dealing with this on a regular basis, you need to refill your cup. For instance, if you are a caregiver, it can be emotionally exhausting, so you have to refill your cup. Take care of yourself and spend some time to reflect on your life.

Practicing other kinds of self-care is also important. You will feel more emotionally resilient when you feel physically and mentally cared for.

Don't interact with them when you are alone

Put limits on how much time you would spend engaging with difficult people who drain your energy. If meeting them is a must, connect with them virtually, schedule something else directly after your meeting with them so that you don't spend much time with them, or you can meet them in a neutral space.

Do your best not to interact with them when you are alone. Go along with a colleague, friend, or someone who can help buffer the interactions you have with them. If the situation starts going the way you don't expect it to go or you notice that you are beginning to get upset, this individual can help you before things become too rough.

Difficult Individuals at the Workplace

Dealing with people who are difficult can be hard enough, but when the difficult person you are dealing with is a coworker, it can ruin your day. A large part of our time is spent at work, so negative people can really take a toll on our productivity, psychological safety, and sense of belonging.

Do your best to reduce your interactions with difficult individuals at work. Whenever appropriate, bring in a third party when you are having difficult conversations. When dealing with your co-workers, try to keep your body language neutral, since additional tension is capable of making the interaction feel more difficult.

If it is one person, such as a manager, that you have to deal with, try to get to the point and keep it brief. Remember that you and the person both have a common interest, which is to get the work done.

You can escalate an existing conflict with a difficult person to HR. While you may not always get along with every individual at work, there are some cases that you should allow human resources to handle. In certain cases, you can reach out to your administrative team, leader, or manager if it feels like things are getting out of control.

When conflicts involve harassment, when it involves inappropriate advances or sexual conduct, when it involves bullying, when it involves violations of equal employment, disability, discrimination, or equal pay laws, or when it involves threats against your family, you, or your livelihood, you should escalate conflicts with coworkers to human resources right away. If you don't feel safe, ensure that you stay away from that co-worker.

Nobody enjoys interacting with difficult individuals, but you don't have to allow it to ruin your day or workplace. While you cannot change their behavior, you can change the way you respond to them and reduce the impact of their behavior on you. You can also practice being more open to conflict and conversation since not every conflict is actually bad.

Your confidence will increase when you learn how to embrace productive conflict and have difficult conversations. As you do this, you might just make a friend in a place you never expected.

CHAPTER THREE
Conflict Resolution Skills

Whatever the cause of disputes or disagreements at work or home may be, there are skills that can help you constructively resolve conflict and keep your relationships strong. You may find yourself weighed down by conflict, but worry no more. Conflict resolution skills can help you resolve any conflict.

Building the following skills will help you:

Leadership and communication skills

A good leader knows what to do to motivate the members of his team and build an atmosphere of collaboration.

Conflict can be prevented and the conflict resolution process facilitated when there is effective communication with your team.

Emotional intelligence and interpersonal skills

Emotional intelligence is a person's ability to perceive emotions in oneself and other individuals and to manage and control the emotions. Conflict resolution requires an understanding of emotions and effective handling of those emotions. Emotional intelligence skills improve relationships and communication, thereby making the skills important for conflict resolution.

Understanding emotional cues and communicating both verbally and nonverbally are important things a manager should be able to do. Emotional intelligence helps when it comes to resolving issues and stopping conflict from escalating. EQ skills are required from all the individuals involved in the conflict, from mediators who use empathy to understand the conflict from different perspectives, and from individuals who are able to set goals that are clear while listening to all the parties' needs for a successful resolution of conflict.

Ensure that you stay calm at all times as a conflict mediator when you are helping other people deal with their emotions. You need to be careful of your interaction with other individuals and set an example as the leader of a team.

Problem-solving skills

Conflict resolution requires problem-solving skills. These skills assist us in recognizing the main causes of conflicts and addressing them by identifying the issues and coming up with solutions. These problem-solving steps can be used by managers to resolve conflict. Individuals can find equitable and creative solutions to the conflicts they have by using problem-solving skills. Problem-solving skills have the ability to determine what is causing the problem and find a solution that is effective. During the resolution of a conflict, a manager might identify areas of compromise between two members of a team who disagree by using their problem-solving skills.

Patience and active listening skills

Although resolving conflict is quite challenging, it is an important part of any relationship. When an argument escalates until things become worse, it can be frustrating. But to successfully resolve conflict, patience is important. Managers don't need to rush into any decision. They need to take their time. When you are trying to resolve a conflict, you need to step back and understand the point of view of the other individual so that you can come up with a solution that will be okay for both parties. When you listen carefully and then think about everything, you can make the situation less tense and trust can be built between you and the other individual. Patience can be a major skill when it comes to the resolution of conflict.

One important skill required for conflict resolution is active listening. It involves focusing on what the other individual is saying and not speaking over them or interrupting them. When you listen actively to the other individual's point of view, it allows them to feel heard and understood, thereby making it easy to resolve the conflict.

Being non-judgmental and open-minded during active listening is also important. When you have an open mind, you are able to explore different ideas and perspectives without taking sides or becoming frustrated. By listening actively and non-defensively, you will easily understand the conflict from the perspective of the other individual and do your best to come up with a solution that works for everyone involved.

Active listening is important for management of conflict and conflict management. If a person's behavior at work is disruptive, a co-worker might approach them, and when the person listens actively, they can gain an understanding of the complaint's origin and how to solve the issue.

Project planning and resource management skills

When you plan your projects, everybody on the team will easily understand their role, and this helps to reduce the chances that there will be a conflict.

When resources are effectively allocated, everybody is able to do their job well. When there is an underallocation of resources, it causes burnout and other problems that might cause conflict to arise in the team.

Negotiation skills

Negotiation involves trying to come to an agreement between two or more parties. It is often used for the resolution of conflicts and disputes and is a major part of conflict resolution. You can learn and practice negotiation skills, and you can apply the skills in various situations. For successful outcomes to be achieved in any situation, having effective negotiation skills is important. One powerful skill used for resolving conflict is negotiation, and it can bring people together to achieve a common goal. Creativity and communication skills are required to negotiate and get problems resolved successfully. Understanding the other party's point of view, listening carefully when they are speaking, and striving to achieve a win-win outcome for all the parties involved should not be ignored.

Mediation skills

The process by which a third party steps in to resolve a dispute between the parties involved is referred to as mediation.

Mediation is an alternative to going to court or litigation, thereby allowing the parties involved to work out their disagreement without the need for a law enforcement officer or judge. The mediator is someone with experience in resolving disputes and is typically impartial. Collaborative mediation, dispute resolution panels, and facilitation are different types of mediation that are available to assist parties in resolving the conflicts that they have.

Mediation makes it possible for a resolution that is acceptable to all parties involved to be reached. It is an important step in the resolution of conflict, as it brings the conflict to the surface so that it is discussed openly to find beneficial and mutually agreeable solutions for everyone involved. Mediation occurs when a neutral third party is involved in a conflict's resolution.

A mediator can be an individual outside the conflict, a person from an outside group, or a skilled professional who can provide an objective perspective. A successful mediator is able to summarize what they are observing and hearing to demonstrate agreement and progress.

Positivity skills

One skill that is required for conflict resolution is positivity. It is important to be constructive and positive when tackling any conflict that arises. Negativity is capable of leading to escalation of conflict and long-term problems. Positive thinking is capable of stopping negative emotions from taking over and preventing you from thinking clearly. You will be able to solve the problem and move ahead with the goals you have. In addition, this attitude will help you achieve the goals you have and a more productive and positive work environment will be created.

Self-awareness skills

Self-awareness is an essential skill for conflict resolution. It makes it easy for you to understand your behavior, feelings, and thoughts, thereby helping you to identify the cause of the conflicts. Once you have a full understanding of what caused the conflict, you can then start using other conflict management techniques and skills to resolve it. You will be able to use self-awareness to identify any biases you have as a manager.

Perspective-taking and responsibility

The ability to understand another individual's point of view is known as perspective-taking. You will need to ask yourself questions about what their thoughts are, what triggers them, and their observations. For instance, a person may call customer service when they are confused about the company's product and don't know how to use the product.

The customer service agent who receives the client's call clearly understands how to use the product and they also benefit from understanding the confusion of the client. In fact, potential improvements to training or product design can be revealed by these conversations.

When it comes to conflict resolution, it is important to hold people responsible for their actions. For instance, there may be a need for a representative from HR to check in a few days later to make sure that every individual is doing what they have agreed to do after an agreement is reached.

Team awareness skills

Team awareness is an important skill for conflict resolution. A conflict resolution team needs to have the skills to collaborate effectively. Managers are able to understand how their team members interact with each other and they also understand their team dynamics as a result of this skill. Also, team awareness is capable of helping with conflict resolution before the issue becomes worse. This skill assists a manager in making the members of their teams work through their differences and arrive at a consensus on a solution.

Observation skills

Observation is important when it comes to managing conflict effectively. When a person observes a conflict, they can properly understand the issue and be able to come up with solutions that work for all the parties involved. You need to be able to watch your emotions and your responses to stay impartial. The kind of conflict you are handling is what will determine the skills you need to be a practical observer.

For instance, if you find yourself involved in a conflict in the workplace, it would be good for you to watch how your colleagues at work interact and solve issues while working as a team. However, if you find yourself involved in a conflict with a friend or family member, observing the individual's body language and non-verbal cues like their tone of voice and facial expressions will be helpful.

Bias for action and facilitation

When a person has a bias for action, it means that they are assertively seeking out the next steps and not waiting for another individual to do something. When it comes to resolution of conflict, this could show up as a colleague at work noticing that they may have made another individual upset and then actively trying to address the issue as soon as possible.

When a manager discovers that there is a conflict, they can also resolve the conflict before it becomes too late to do anything. You can arrange the environment around you when there is conflict to make resolution easier. For instance, a manager who is in charge of overseeing two different groups can get the groups to discuss what they disagree about on a joint project together in a comfortable conference room. Providing space and time for discussion can make the conflict quickly come to an end.

CHAPTER FOUR
The Resolution Process

You can use conflict resolution strategies to resolve, control, and prevent conflicts as a mediator. Conflict resolution processes work differently for different teams or organizations. There is not a single one that works for them all. However, many teams or organizations follow a similar conflict resolution process. We will discuss conflict resolution in the workplace after this. However, you can use the following steps in any area of your life and they will work for you.

Let us take a look at these steps of the conflict resolution process:

First Step: Acknowledge the existence of the problem

Proceed with the conflict resolution by accepting the existence of a problem. At first, you may be thinking that the people involved are overdoing things and making a mountain out of a molehill. But you need to consider the fact that something that may seem insignificant to you may be seen as a big issue by another individual.

The lens through which you are viewing the problem should be shifted. Ensure that you do your best to adopt a positive outlook when it comes to embracing conflicts of all complexities and sizes. Don't see this as a burden, but consider it an opportunity for every individual involved to learn, develop, and grow.

Second Step: Define behavior that is acceptable

Before you even notice any conflict, you can eliminate or reduce potential issues by setting a standard of behavior that the workplace should have. If you give the team a chance to define what is appropriate and what is not, they will.

However, your responsibility as a manager is to set the tone. This can be done by coming up with a framework for how discussions are run, writing specific job descriptions, noting the hierarchy and which individual is responsible for what, defining the proper practices for business, selecting which project management tools to use, and assisting with leadership development and team building, and so on. As you set more guidelines, the team gets better at following them.

You can establish guidelines in this beginning stage. Let all the parties involved know that you are all about to find a solution that will be beneficial to everyone. Emphasize that if anybody breaks the rules, you will put off the meeting until they can behave well.

Some of the rules may include:

- No cursing, threatening, or yelling.
- Calmly express yourself.
- Try to gain an understanding of other people's points of view.
- No use of passive-aggressive comments.

Is this a straight-up harassment or conflict?

You need to understand harassing behaviors better.

Third Step: Don't turn a blind eye to conflict

You can respond to conflict in the workplace in several ways, depending on the type of manager and person you are. You could decide to ignore the conflict and allow the participants to handle it themselves. This approach is not the worst one. Conflict resolution is one tool that teams need for effective collaboration.

However, if you are trying not to deal with conflict because it makes you feel uncomfortable or because you don't want to reprimand an individual, then you are getting it wrong. Of course, you are meant to handle such issues as a manager. You have the power to act when the situation demands it and you should act when necessary. If you don't do this, the situation might get worse and even negatively affect the business.

Fourth Step: Choose a place that is neutral

You need to first change the environment to diffuse the conflict. When people are heated, the anger is usually tied to a place. This sounds odd, but the conflict will be put into perspective when people are taken away from the room where they are fighting.

You can take the individuals who are upset to a neutral location to resolve the conflict. When you are in a neutral space, things are brought down to a level in which you can have a constructive conversation. When you suggest a place outside the office, such as a coffee house, where there is no power dynamic, a comfortable atmosphere will be created where the cause of the issue can be productively dealt with.

Fifth Step: Give compliments

After you have left the place where the conflict started, you can tackle the problem. You don't have to go into a conversation with an accusatory tone. You need to hear all sides of the story and make the right decision based on the needs of the work being done and the facts. Therefore, to make an individual comfortable enough to open up and talk about the issue, you need to start by complimenting them. Show them that there is no good guy or bad guy here. You are there to attack the problem, not the individual.

Sixth Step: Avoid jumping to conclusions

What causes conflict is usually more complex than it seems at first. Ensure that you do not jump to conclusions as you have to treat all parties involved fairly. Give every individual a chance to share their side of the story even if you think the conflict is obvious. You need to first understand the history involved. You should not be assuming anything about any individual. Get your facts right and then make a wise decision.

Seventh Step: Find out the cause of the conflict

Before you continue, you need to first know what the conflict is and understand what is causing the problem.

It is important that you listen to what the two parties involved are saying about the incident when you are handling a conflict among team members. You can use the techniques of root cause analysis for conflicts that are more complex and involve lots of contributing factors and causes.

When you have more information about what is causing the problem, you will be able to easily resolve it. You can ask questions to help you identify the cause of the problem and use the right resolution strategies to solve the problem. You can ask questions like, "How did the conflict start?" "When did you start getting upset?" "Do you see a connection between that and this issue?" These questions will help you in identifying the root cause of the conflict.

As a supervisor or manager, you need to allow both parties involved the opportunity to share their own side of the story. It will help you understand the situation better and also help you show your impartiality. As the parties talk about the dispute, you can acknowledge the information they are giving you and then encourage them to talk more about everything.

Open the communication lines for conflicting parties to talk about the issue without outbursts or interruptions. Allow both parties that are involved in the conflict to talk informally, but do your best to monitor the discussion and make sure that there is adequate time for each party to speak.

Don't allow the conversation to be monopolized by one person and don't start sharing your own point of view until both parties that are involved in the conflict have had an opportunity to express their feelings, concerns, and thoughts.

A lot of emotion is bound to be present in these conversations, meaning that it is easy for them to go off course, thereby hindering progress. The dialogue can quickly be pushed into a toxic place by the intensity between the conflicted parties.

A mediator who is skillful will keep reminding them that the conflict has already occurred and that this discussion is meant to tackle the conflict, and not to attack each other. You can use these conflict resolution strategies to keep the dialogue on track.

Pay attention and listen for ultimatums, threats, intimidation, scare tactics, bullying, or aggression. If you see that the discussion is becoming aggressive and not assertive, you can assist the speaker with communicating their position. Coercive offers and threats might temporarily stop the problem, but the solution is not a long-term one. Put your focus on the issue at hand.

The conversation should not be focused on the individual but on the problem. Although the parties who are in conflict may feel like attacking each other, you must try to get them to focus on the primary goal of the conversation.

Constantly check your own pre-conceived attitudes also. Understand that you should be maintaining a perspective that is bias-free. Sometimes the individual is the issue in a conflict, but try to look at other causes before considering that.

Ask the individuals involved in the conflict to use "I" statements. When using "I" statements, the individual does not blame the other party but frames thoughts around themselves. You can say something like, "I felt embarrassed and confused when I led the project meeting myself, instead of "You are always coming late to meetings."

Encourage the individuals to use storytelling when having a productive discussion. When you are retelling events without emotions, a clear timeline, and details, the listener can be pushed to become indifferent and not sympathetic. When you tell stories, you create a clearer picture that can be easily acknowledged and understood.

Eighth Step: Active listening

Actively listen to the conversation and encourage the party who is not speaking to also listen actively. Don't interrupt when someone is speaking. Ask for clarification and feedback to ensure that everyone understands everything clearly.

Many active listening techniques exist, but the following are the best:

Give your full attention

Offer the speaker your undivided attention, then make them see that you are present in the conversation. Offer small encouragement or nod along as you listen to show them that you are hearing what they are saying and understanding it.

Do not interrupt

It is important that you allow others to speak. Do not interrupt them when they are speaking. As part of a welcoming and open conversation, every individual must be allowed to share their own side of the story without any disruptions or fear.

Don't be afraid of silence

Some people see silence as embarrassing, confusing, or awkward. Silence is beneficial in difficult conversations. When you pause instead of speaking, all the parties involved get a chance to reflect on the conversation and think about what to say next.

Ninth Step: Reach a complete understanding

The aim is to reach a full understanding of the conflict as well as the different perspectives. You need to make sure that all the parties involved are on the same page.

After listening to each party explaining their side, you need to evaluate, investigate, and analyze both sides. Don't just make assumptions or jump to conclusions. Take time to study the situation and make the right decision.

Repeat each account's highlights and restate the issues so that the parties are given a chance to correct you if you are not understanding everything well. Ask questions so that you can be clear about certain things if that will help.

Make an attempt to bring up any deeper issues that exist beneath the surface. Differentiate between circumstantial values and non-negotiable values.

Tenth Step: Understand what both parties want

What usually causes anger to fester is not the situation itself but the point of view of the parties involved, which may ultimately result in a shouting match.

Once you completely understand the nature of the conflict and what caused it, the next thing to do is to identify what both parties want from the resolution process, which will involve coming up with a solution that both parties will accept.

The cause of the conflict in the workplace might be a small issue that occurred weeks before, but the stress level has increased to the point where the two parties involved in the situation have started attacking each other personally and not addressing the issue. When you are alone, take some time to study the situation and see the real cause. You will find probing questions helpful as they will help ease the disagreement and help you come up with a solution for the problem.

When your management skills are improved, you will be able to effectively manage conflict situations and identify triggers even before conflict arises. You will also gain credibility and trust with your employees.

Eleventh Step: Identify barriers to conflict resolution

Before looking for a solution, take some time to identify conflict resolution barriers that might slow down the process of conflict resolution and do your best to eliminate the barriers.

Twelveth Step: Select a style for the conflict resolution

Consider the previous steps we have discussed to choose the conflict resolution style that fits your situation. In some situations, there might be a need to tell someone that they are wrong, build a solution that is a win-win for both parties, or find a middle ground that is satisfactory. Do this analysis on a case-by-case basis.

Thirteenth Step: Offer guidance and provide constructive criticism

One other thing to know as you handle conflict in your workplace or anywhere is not to jump straight away to just righting the wrong. This means that there could be something obvious that is causing the conflict and a clear way to get the individuals involved back on the same page and to do their work productively.

You are the group's leader and you are not meant to take sides in the arguments they are having. Getting the team to work together to get the conflict resolved is the best thing to do. That means you have to take more time to lead them to the right conclusion, even though they may be too emotional to do the right thing.

While consequences are required by some conflicts, most conflicts start when passionate people handle a situation from different points of view. The opportunity to learn or teach truth also arises when conflicts arise. A manager uses the conflicts as a means to address what has been causing problems for the team.

A multitude of approaches exist in any conflict, and some approaches are more critical than others. But sometimes, you will notice that things are simply wrong, and the only valid way to deal with the situation is through criticism. However, you have to understand that you will still continuously work with the same individuals you are criticizing. So, to criticize and still lead effectively, you have to criticize without embittering. And how can you do that? This is where you need to use constructive criticism. This approach helps you to blame and address the issue, but also acknowledge the good work the individuals have already done. You give them guidance so that the issue can be solved. Nobody is resentful and the team now has the necessary tools to avoid repeating what caused the problem.

Fourteenth Step: Avoid intimidating anyone

You are in a position of authority as a manager, so ensure that you don't abuse it. Intimidation might seem like what you need to do to fix the problem, but doing this means that you are only thinking in the short term. The members of the team will be afraid of you, but they will not learn anything from this. This means that whenever something goes wrong, they will leave you in the dark and will not confide in you. This can make the issue get out of hand and it will be too late to fix it before you even notice it. So, ensure that you take time to work through your conflict resolution so that it doesn't come up again after the problem has been solved.

Fifteenth Step: Look for a viable solution

After you have implemented a conflict management style, you need to have a solution that is viable and solves the conflict. After understanding each of the party's viewpoints, you can then ask them to identify how the situation could be changed. Ask the conflicting parties questions again to get ideas from them. "What can you do to make things better between you and the other individual?" You need to be an active listener and be great at reading body language when you are managing conflict as a mediator.

You want both parties to stop fighting and start working together in harmony, and that means moving the discussion toward the direction of resolving the conflict.

You are paying attention to everything and listening for the course of action that is most acceptable. Make both disputants see the advantages of various ideas and how the ideas benefit the organization, and not just see things from each other's perspective. For example, you might suggest that they should collaborate and cooperate more to be able to effectively address departmental problems and team issues.

Before any solution is implemented, make sure that the participants of the conflict are in agreement with the solution and committed to it.

Sixteenth Step: Make a decision

Remember, time is needed to properly resolve conflict. But it is now time to act after you have gone through the steps above, and you should act decisively.

Don't waste time before making the decision so that you don't leave the team confused. It makes you appear to be a bad leader. You are creating a void, which will get filled by ideas that are not yours, and the authority you need to lead may be lost. So, you need to act on a decision when you come to it. Some people might not like it, but this will let them know where you stand.

For conflict resolution in the workplace, you need to acknowledge the feelings that were hurt and the situation. You also need to identify a solution that fixes the damage that has been done and prevents harm in the future and then implement that solution.

To have an effective resolution, you need to make it as fast as possible. Once all the details have been gathered, you have discussed with all the parties, listened to all sides of the story, and fully understood everything, you can then make a decision.

Neglecting to come up with a decision or leaving a conflict in limbo can cause damage to your credibility and make you appear incompetent and insensitive. It also makes the conflict to worsen.

A successful mediator is able to diffuse the conflict and decide on how best to resolve the issue. You can use strong internal policies to nip conflict in the bud.

Seventeenth Step: Arrive at a negotiated agreement

The mediator's job after coming up with a solution to the problem is to get both parties to shake hands and agree to one of the alternatives that have been presented. The aim is to arrive at a negotiated agreement. What some mediators do is go as far as to draw up a contract in which the actions to take and the time frames to perform them are specified. However, meeting with both parties and asking them some questions is okay. Ask them questions about what they will do to prevent conflicts in the future, and what they will do if they experience problems in the future. You can use this mediation process for individuals as well as groups.

Eighteenth Step: Follow up

When the conversation comes to an end, thank each of the parties involved for taking part in the conversation and acknowledge that progress has been made.

Reach out to them at a later date and ensure that you use the method that is the most appropriate. Based on the status of the resolution and the conflict itself, that might need to be a call, an email, or a face-to-face conversation.

Ensure that you restate the resolution and thank the parties again during this follow-up. If you are in a position to give advice and it is appropriate, do so. Make them understand that you are available to discuss any issues they have or any future thoughts.

The process of conflict resolution should not end once the conflict has been solved by finding a solution. Remember to follow up with the members of the team to make sure that the conflict has ended and everything has been successfully resolved.

Nineteenth Step: Prevent future reoccurrence

You can carefully screen all the employees during the hiring process, take all the necessary precautions, and give them as much training as possible, but you need to understand that full-day workshops and polished interview responses won't guarantee a workplace that is healthy.

After the conflict has been resolved, you need to do your best to prevent it from happening again by taking the necessary next steps. Necessary action items may include adding an employee manual or a behavioral statement to your code of conduct, or clarifying roles if that was causing problems. You can start by forming a culture that promotes honest and open conversations. Encourage everyone to be transparent in their dealings so that unpleasant truths can disappear before they become intense conflicts.

Managing and Resolving Conflict at Work

Conflict is not new to most people. Many individuals experience it in their everyday lives with their families and friends and in their professional lives. Conflict in the workplace can result in a massive degree of discomfort, pain, sadness, anger, and frustration. There is bound to be conflict because organizations hire employees from different intellectual and cultural backgrounds, different geographical locations, and various viewpoints. For this reason, disagreements are bound to happen as people can have different views about a particular problem.

We know that people will always experience conflict at one point or the other in their lives. So, the idea is not to try to stop conflict from happening, but to resolve and manage it effectively if it happens. When individuals address issues with the appropriate tools for resolution, they will be able to manage their differences so that major problems are not caused. It is important to establish conflict management processes in an organization as it assists in reducing instances of conflict among co-workers.

Any individual in management, especially people who have become managers newly needs the skill of handling disputes efficiently, and they also need to be able to prevent disputes from negatively affecting the professional growth of employees.

Conflict resolution helps to distinguish between good and bad businesses, therefore it is important in the corporate world. So, what are the steps you should take to resolve conflict as a business owner?

Resolving conflicts in the workplace is possible by doing the following:

Gain clarity about the source of the conflict

The first thing to do when it comes to resolving conflict in the workplace is to first clarify the source of the conflict. You need to first find the source of the conflict as this is very important when it comes to solving any problem. When you define the cause of the problem, you will be able to understand how the problem started and grew to the present state. Also, you will be able to bring both parties who are involved in the conflict to agree to what their disagreement is. To achieve this, you will need to discuss the needs, which both sides are not meeting. In addition, you need to ensure that there is mutual understanding and get as much information as possible from each of the sides. Ask questions continuously until you are sure that everyone involved understands the issue. Identifying the root cause of the problem and ensuring that it will not happen again is crucial.

Get a private and safe place to talk

Many individuals usually wonder and ask, "What approach should be used to peacefully solve problems?" You need to look for a safe environment where you can have a constructive conversation. This place also makes you take the risks that are necessary to have honest communication concerning the current issues to be resolved.

So, before you start trying to resolve the problem, ensure that you get a private and safe place to talk. Do not go to the office of any of the parties or any location that is close to them. While you are at this place, each party should be given enough time to speak and air out their concerns regarding the issue.

Allow every individual to have their say

After you have invited both parties involved in the conflict to meet in a private and secure place, give each of them the opportunity to air out their perceptions and views concerning the problem. Give each of the parties equal time to express their concerns and thoughts without favoring one side over the other. Welcome an assertive and positive approach while in the meeting. Set ground rules if necessary. Using this approach will help both parties to articulate their thoughts in an honest and open manner, and also comprehend the conflict's causes, and identify solutions to the problem.

Investigate the case

After both parties have spoken, it is then time for you to investigate the case. Do not make assumptions or settle on a final verdict based on what you have. Go deeper and get more information about the parties involved, the conflict, the feelings of people, and everything happening. Have a confident and individual conversation with the people involved and listen attentively to ensure you clearly understand their viewpoints. This can be done by summarizing what they have said and repeating it to them. Also, look for any underlying sources of conflict which may be invisible or not evident at first.

Look for ways to meet the goals of all the parties

You need to have a common objective when you are managing conflict processes. The objective should be to resolve the problem and ensure that it does not resurface.

To manage any problem, you have to be aware of the conflict's different stages. This will help you to look for the best ways to meet the goals of all the parties involved. After clarifying the conflict's source, hearing from both parties and doing an investigation about the conflict, you need to discuss with both parties involved and talk about ways you can use to achieve the common goal, which is resolving the issue at hand. Listen to everyone, communicate with them, and brainstorm together until you look at all the available options.

Determine each party's responsibilities

Communication is important when it comes to managing and resolving conflict.

It will be easy for employees to interact with one another as they get to understand that they are working towards one goal, which is achieving the objectives of the company. So, after you have investigated the situation and looked for ways through which you can solve the problem, both parties need to come to a final conclusion on the best solution for the issue. And you need to find solutions that each of the parties involved can live with so that you can agree on the best. You need to look for a common ground. After that, determine each party's responsibilities in resolving the issue.

Prevent the issue from resurfacing in the future

Never assume things about the conflict. Effective communication should dominate in the business. So, you need to ask yourself the question, "What is effective communication's second step?" and "What type of internal communication does the organization have?" When you know this, it ensures that the workers are working together to meet the goals of the organization. So, ensure that you keep an eye on the issue and check to see if the solution you have come up with is effective. If the issue comes back again, you need to take the necessary action.

In addition, you need to decide on strategies that will help to prevent the issue from resurfacing in the future. Many individuals usually ask, "What conflict occurs every day?" Some individuals may not have the same opinion on everything, and this may be a problem. So, pay attention and check for any lessons you can learn from the problem and what you can do to fix the problem. This will make it possible for you to know what you can do when the problem comes up again and also help you develop and grow your conflict management skills.

Conflict is inevitable in our everyday lives. You can disagree with your co-workers, friends, or family. But, different conflict resolution steps exist that you can use to manage the issue. Resolving conflict that occurs at work is important when it comes to meeting the goals of the organization. So, if there are any disagreements between your employers or you have any issues, look for ways to manage the situation. These techniques and tips that we have discussed can help you in resolving conflicts in the workplace.

CHAPTER FIVE
Successful Negotiations

People have negotiations every day in their businesses and in their lives generally. While some negotiations are small, some are big. But one common thing about negotiation whether it is big or small is the aim, which is to find the best situation for all parties involved in the negotiation.

Now, the outcome of negotiating with your partner over which of the movies you should watch is not very important. You can just allow the negotiation to go in any direction it is going. This is because no matter what happens, you will still have a good time together.

But, if you are someone in charge of a major negotiation, it is serious and you can't just leave things to chance. In fact, many practices and principles exist which apply to most cases and they can be used consistently.

Negative images of conflict and struggle can be conjured up by the word "negotiation." But successful negotiation has to do with discussion that is meant to reach an agreement.

A good negotiator doesn't use aggression to reach a deal; they use skillful techniques to do it. While practice is required to develop negotiation skills, becoming great at negotiation is possible. Only some basic guidelines that are based on the ultimate goal are required to successfully reach an agreement that both parties will accept.

So, are you interested in knowing the steps that you can take and have successful negotiations?

Following these steps will help you achieve the most out of every negotiation you do and you will achieve success:

Know what is at stake and define your goals

Individuals who are great at negotiating know what they want before starting a discussion. They know the things they will and will not accept. Successful negotiators have a point when they walk away. So, if you cannot walk away when the need arises, you are getting set to make a bad deal.

Also, you need to know that you are not going to win every point. Make a decision about what parts you are willing to concede and what parts are important. And ensure that you never, ever concede beyond the point where you have decided to walk away. It is better to lose a bad deal than to make a bad deal.

The most important step when it comes to making a successful negotiation is to properly set your goals. You need to know what your ideal scenario is and also what is at stake.

The other individual might not agree to whatever you are asking them for. So, even though you know what your best option is, you also need to know what you can compromise on. What you need to do here is to define well in advance the lowest you are willing to accept. And then never go below that point.

Moreover, when you are defining the goals that you have, you need to ensure that you don't consider only the immediate needs that you have. Instead, look at the future and these factors should be included in your strategy. If you understand what is at stake and what you are standing for, it will be easy for you to come up with solid arguments.

Do proper research and prepare for the negotiation

Get yourself armed with factual information before entering into a negotiation. Gather as much information as possible that is relevant to your negotiations. This involves asking yourself some questions as well. What is the reason why you want to do this deal? What made the other party want to do the deal? What will everyone gain from this deal? Then do your best to get information that benefits your position as well as theirs. Having all the facts makes you confident and gives you a position of strength.

Information is important, especially when it comes to negotiation. Proper research is one important thing you need to do to boost your chances of achieving success. Ensure that you get enough information about the individual you are negotiating with. What hurdles are their business facing? Try to find out the challenges and what could be expected from the negotiation. Check for the available options. Check out industry and business news. Get some more information about the other party.

Ensure that you do not rush to make conclusions that may affect you negatively in the future, but preparation will help you direct the conversation the way you want it to go. You will be able to ask questions that are more targeted and gain more information. The research you make will help to put you in a position that will get you closer to your ideal scenario.

Identify the person with the authority

Before you dive into your negotiation, you need to ensure that you are actually in contact with the individual who has the authority to make the business decisions. This step is crucial because you might find that you have wasted time trying to get a deal with an individual who does not have the power to say yes to the deal.

Sometimes, you may not know any individual from the organization you want to approach, but you can find a lot of information online. Check the organization's online presence and look at the organization's leaders. It can help you know the individual in charge of signing or approving business contracts.

If you don't find that information on the company's website and you decide to go directly to the company, the first person you might come in contact with is the gatekeeper. A first impression is important and will decide whether or not you will be given a chance for a meeting. Do the best you can do to leave a good impression on the company's gatekeeper.

If you find it hard to reach any individual at the company, you can leverage your network. Do you know any individual who has a connection at the company you are trying to reach? If there is any mutual connection, you will find them beneficial as a first contact point. You may get referred to the decision maker or get some valuable feedback.

Ensure that you build trust

Trust is the next thing on the list of what is required for negotiations to be successful. In fact, being sure of this is very important in negotiations. The outcome of the conversation will be influenced by the attitude you have towards your opponent.

Start the talk by approaching it from a win-win angle. For that reason, it is important for trust to be built on the interpersonal level. It will assist you in working together towards an agreement that is satisfactory.

Meetings that are held face-to-face are far more profitable in this sense. You can use video chats to share ideas and know the individual better if this is not possible. Ask questions that have to do with personal matters. What makes them get out of bed every day and do the things they need to do?

Look for common ground while discussing interests, passions, hobbies, or even dislikes. Ensure that you ask the other individual about their wants, needs, and pressures as well. They have these wants, needs, and pressures. And you will start to build trust and some positive vibe if you show them that you care about also meeting the requirements that they have.

Just as you desire to get information concerning your counterpart, you need to make sure that no valuable information is kept for yourself. Stay willing and open to sharing personal and business information.

Don't take no for an answer

A certain level of assertiveness is required for negotiations. As a business person, you should know that most things are negotiable. So, ask for what you want, and don't be shy to ask. Be persistent and refuse to take no for an answer. Explain clearly what you hope to achieve, but ensure that you explain in a peaceful and empathic way. Respect the interests of other individuals and avoid displaying aggressive behavior.

Practice can be done anytime by you. Reflect on the way you are making your arguments. Focus more on "I" statements. You can say. "I am not comfortable with this," instead of saying "You should stop…"

Double-check information. Do not jump to accept every piece of information without thinking about it critically. Ensure that you question requirements like a fixed price, and so on. Pay attention to the arguments of your opponent, reflect on the arguments, and then take time to prepare counter-arguments.

Ensure that you also communicate what you can do to satisfy the necessary requirements. The more heard and pleased they feel with your proposal, the more likely they will give you an offer that is satisfying.

Don't feel obliged to accept the offer instantly

An offer will be made by your counterpart but you don't have to feel obliged to make a decision instantly. Spend time and think about it. If you are not sure about it and you want to accept the offer because you just want to close a deal, you will probably regret the decision you are making later.

Instead, ensure that you prepare a counteroffer that is based on your needs and goals. It is definitely preferred to get a quick deal. However, a cooling-off period is not bad. Fresh ideas will come up and you can have a reflection on the things that have happened.

At best, you will start on the right note. If not, don't forget that you can walk away whenever you want. Cutting ties completely is not what you have to do because you may have a new opportunity in the future to cooperate.

Ask the right questions

The next thing to do for a successful negotiation is to ask questions. If you are a business person, you know how valuable relevant information about your counterpart is.

That is why it is important to have the right questions in mind. You need to think carefully about how you ask your questions in advance, as the outcome can be radically changed by the way you ask. Some individuals might view it as an art, but the reality is that you can get prepared and ensure that you keep things under control.

Whenever possible, try to avoid questions that have to do with yes or no which are usually not very effective. Stay focused on open questions to maximize the input of information. Questions that have to do with "what," "when", "how," or "who" call for you to be given a more detailed answer. Leading questions can be used to get individuals towards your point of view.

Is there something you need to know? Ask the person you are having a conversation with how they feel about the points that have been discussed.

Ensure that you formulate clear questions that will reveal your counterpart's desires and needs.

Show your passion

It is important to show when you are satisfied with something. How does the proposal make you feel? Your conversation partner should know this. A great way to reinforce your dissent or agreement on a topic is body language.

If you are happy about the proposition of the opponent, you can express it to them in words and wearing a smile on your face. When you want to show your dissatisfaction, the same thing applies. Disagreement should be stressed with an explanation and the power of facial expressions can be used to convey it.

Displaying emotions can be something powerful. It shows that you care about the topic of negotiation and both positions. And always remember to have the right balance between emotionally guided and rational actions.

It will be easier for you to connect with people if you convince them by using your passion.

Start with high expectations

Begin the negotiation with requirements that are higher than you would expect. This can make your counterpart focus more on arguments that are in support of the initial value. They will even make suggestions around it.

During the conversation, the claims decrease regularly. In any situation, this approach provides you room for reducing prices as well as other parameters.

Nonetheless, you are still more likely to leave satisfied so it is good to start high.

If you maintain an optimistic attitude, a positive outcome can also be achieved. On the other hand, if you start with low expectations, you may find yourself having unsatisfying results.

Give the other individual fair treatment

Data from research provides an interesting revelation concerning negotiations. There are many times when a negotiation has broken down because one of the parties thinks that the other party wasn't giving them fair treatment. What exactly does this mean? It means that rational discussion was overcome by ego and emotions. When you hit your hand on the table and give an ultimatum, it may make for a great stage play or a great theater in a movie. But these things hardly get deals in real life. Stay respectful, keep a cool head, and treat other individuals the way you want to be treated. These things will help this deal get done and also present you as a fair dealer by the time another negotiation comes.

Look for a win-win scenario

Very often, people consider negotiation to be a zero-sum game. They believe that one party must win and the other must lose. People who are successful when it comes to negotiation see it as an opportunity for both parties to win. For instance, during the negotiation of a salary, the employee wants to be given an amount that is higher than the offered amount, but the employer does not find the salary flexible. Exploring creative solutions to fill the gap is a way to create a win-win scenario. Perhaps the organization can provide graduate school tuition, daycare reimbursement, flexible work hours, and so on that are of great value to the employee but don't cost much.

Reach an agreement

All of the excellent tactics, strategies, and planning that the most skillful negotiator employs are meaningless if there is no agreement. This can occur when the other party is unable to arrive at a decision. As a negotiator, you should stay prepared for indecision in advance. The decision should be made part of the negotiation, and you need to do it early in the process. A timeline should be set, the criteria should be discussed, and the hurdles that might cause delays when it comes to getting a final agreement approved should be mapped out and implemented.

Practice

You need to practice when it comes to negotiations. It is important that you practice continuously. So, get yourself mentally prepared and set your interview intentions. Plan carefully.

Do you ever remember having negative thoughts in your mind while getting ready for your negotiations? Every one of us experiences these emotions more or less often.

When next you find these feelings stuck in your head, all you have to do is to rephrase your thoughts. Use positive phrases such as "remain confident" and not statements such as "don't mess everything up." Your self-confidence can be boosted by a positive mindset.

If your days are spent in a traditional work environment, there will be several occasions where you will practice for upcoming negotiations. Those situations can include the ones where you need to assign tasks to your co-workers. Or maybe you want to focus on your core work and want other individuals to do other things. There are good negotiation exercises. If things do not work out the way you planned, you can try another strategy the next time.

You get excellent opportunities in life to put your negotiating skills to the test.

You need to put on a smart argument to convince your counterpart. Are you arguing about the best movie for the next night you will go out to the movies? Or are you arguing about who is cooking tonight?

Everyday situations give you the opportunity to improve your negotiating skills. Your stress and risk level will be low, but it makes you practice daily.

You need a mind map to manage your negotiation. It can be used to brainstorm your plan in advance, and you can use it to track progress. The timeline feature can also be used to create deadlines and set milestones.

Basic and Complex Negotiation Tactics

Negotiators who are less experienced may discover that they are tempted to use clever tactics to try to outsmart the party across the table or to stay focused on claiming instead of creating value during a negotiation. However heavy-handed and aggressive maneuvers hardly generate the outcome that individuals hope they will generate. Successful veteran negotiators are aware that the most important thing is mastering the basics of negotiating first, doing effective preparation ahead of time in order to completely understand their counterparts, and staying focused on building a rapport.

Here are what you need for a good negotiation, and some complex tactics as well:

Know what you want

Preparation is important for every negotiation. However, any individual who has ever prepared for negotiation is aware that it is actually more tricky than it appears because it is almost impossible to think about every potentiality that may arise in a situation that is changing quickly.

Follow this to-do list to prepare yourself without getting overwhelmed:

- Identify what you consider success to be to avoid setting the bar too low instead of staying focused on what you think the other party will agree to. You don't have to define the likely outcome but define your jackpot.

- Define everything and the terms you can use when the negotiation is going on and consider new factors that you can talk about.
- Your interests should be defined. You need to know what your priorities are, what you can trade off to achieve your priorities, and how much you can trade off.
- Define the point at which you will walk away. You or your organization will simply not accept some trade-offs and it should be very clear ahead of time.

You should be aware of the weighted value of each of the terms you are negotiating. Identifying specific metrics for achieving success is best. If every negotiable term were considered in a complex negotiation, you might find yourself handling millions of possible combinations. But you need to at least take a look at the items that are at the top of your list, consider your time value of money, and come up with other estimates and create sales. Psychological effects will be minimized by this and the decisions for both sides will also be rationalized, thereby increasing the acceptance likelihood.

After you have created your own list, you need to define each of the items present in the list above for the other individual or party as best you can. You will be better prepared when going for the negotiation if you spend more time thinking about what the other party wants and needs than you think about your wants and needs.

Establish openness and trust

When you are starting a negotiation, let the other side know your priorities and ask them to be open about their priorities. This appears counterintuitive; a lot of people are afraid of sharing that information because they fear that the information will be abused by the other party. Some studies suggest that complete transparency can result in manipulative tactics. However, when you reveal your interest, it can show cooperation as well as elicit reciprocity. If information is offered by the other party, it should empower you to share more. The priorities of your counterpart will provide you with important information that you might not have received during preparation and can result in the discovery of potential concessions and trade-offs.

This is usually overlooked during negotiations because both parties usually believe they want to get a better price and they also focus only on getting the better price. Ensure that you do not talk about price when the negotiation is just beginning so that the optimal outcome can be generated. The toughest item should be left for last.

Building rapport with the other party is what a good negotiation starts with. Trust is important, and great negotiators do their best to establish ground rules about openness as well as trying to get mutual gains. If a particular negotiation is beginning to go awry, you can always decrease the tension by referring to the objectives stated when the process was beginning.

Stay focused on enlarging the pie

Doing a negotiation, as opposed to haggling or bargaining, is capable of creating new value instead of just distributing it. Trades, which involves asking for what you want and giving back something in return, creates new value. When you have several negotiation issues that you can trade, it assists in ensuring that you can enlarge the pie instead of cutting thinner slices of the pie during the negotiation process.

Know how to handle bullying

It is likely that you will meet with a negotiator at some point in your career who tries to claim value in a hostile manner. The individual may use threats and may try to bully you. Fear usually kicks in when that happens and the amygdala, which is the brain's prehistoric part takes over, shutting down the mind's creative parts and getting you prepared for fight or flight. There will be a need for you to buy yourself time to leave this state.

You can start leading the conversation and also get back your ability to think clearly by using simple tools such as questions. For instance, if the other party makes a statement, you may find it helpful to change the statement's last few words and turn it into a question. Even if you notice that you are scared at that moment, the other party will now have to explain more about their statement. That allows you more time to recuperate.

Another effective method that you will find helpful when you use it during these kinds of fraught moments is labeling. When an individual raises their voice, you might tell them that you sense some heightened emotions. That can prompt the other side to end their tirade and then begin to explain, thereby deescalating the situation.

If you are able to use the basic negotiation approaches we talked about above well, your effectiveness will be more than that of eighty percent of negotiators. After you have perfected the use of these basics, including mastering how to build rapport and trust, you can put your focus on some tactics that are advanced, like the ones we will discuss below. Although these tactics can be effective, you should ensure that you use them with caution.

Here are some advanced negotiation tactics:

Establishing a point of reference

Anchoring or establishing a point of reference for the negotiation should be used carefully even though it appears to be a simple tactic. It can also backfire even though it can work even on negotiators who are the most seasoned. If you are thinking about whether you should let the other party go first or make the first offer, you can allow the party with more market information to go first. If you are the individual with more market information, should you ask for something realistic or should you ask for more than you expect so that you can meet in the middle? An anchor that is unrealistic can make the relationship that you have been taking your time to build deteriorate, create hostility, or force the other party to walk away. It is possible for the other party to ask for much less than they could have received from the negotiation, and this is a costly mistake.

In addition, you need to be able to dislodge an anchor that is unrealistic and you should not make a counteroffer that is immediate. That can get the alignment and good rapport that you have established destroyed. If the anchor you are presented with is unrealistic, it is best to let them know that it is a nonstarter and ensure that before you make another offer, both sides realign on strategy.

Deploying multiple equivalent simultaneous offers

You can plan multiple equivalent simultaneous offers if you have properly prepared and listed all the items for your negotiation. For instance, you might give someone two different options in a salary negotiation, in which one of the options has a salary that is lower and has more options for stock or it might be vice versa. You have created new value in the negotiation if you consider both choices equally valuable to you and then the individual for the job picks the one he values more. This also provides you with information about the priorities of the candidate that you can use as you negotiate subsequent items in their employment contract. The items can include retirement benefits, travel expectations, and vacation. It can be tricky to use multiple equivalent simultaneous offers in complex negotiations, but they can be effective when it comes to signaling cooperative intentions and they can be helpful for pros.

What makes a good negotiation is being genuinely interested in the other party and the priorities they have and coming up with fresh issues that you can negotiate over and then have the pie expanded. Rather than getting tempted to use threats to intimidate the other party or to try to outsmart them, make preparation a priority and use the time-tested principles that have been discussed above to create better outcomes in your negotiations.

CHAPTER SIX
The Psychology of Negotiation

A complex skill set is required for negotiating. You need to navigate between the other party's goals and interests and your own goals and interests. You need to be very flexible at the same time. You also need to be able to find the right balance between being assertive and cooperative.

There is usually an overload of information during negotiations; people are not as rational as they think they are and they try to reduce the negotiation's complexity by depending on speculations, decisions taken on reflex, or previous experiences. These incorrect decisions can be prevented by recognizing these pitfalls and learning from them.

Rational arguments cannot make you win negotiations. You will have a much better chance when you use the correct psychological insights. During the process of negotiating, your knowledge of human nature undergoes constant testing. Are you able to assess what the other negotiators feel and think? Are the negotiators interested in the proposal you brought? How much are the negotiators willing to give in? Are they playing a game, or are they serious?

Let us take a look at the familiar tips concerning negotiating:

- Get to know the individual who is your adversary and begin with small talk. When having any negotiation, you will find personal contact important, because you build trust. A personal connection produces great results.
- Simultaneously make a negotiation about more than one area and discriminate between what you need and what you want.

- Work on your negotiation power. Don't stop in the middle and don't go below what you are willing to accept.
- Get to know about the other negotiator's interests and objectives. Try to gain an understanding of these, remain respectful, and separate your negotiations from your emotions.
- Do your best to find a win-win solution, something that is acceptable to both parties.

Working towards a win-win situation is good. Ensure that you never push too hard, and so on. Tensions rise when in negotiations, emotions have the upper hand, and parties eventually go for their own interests.

Dirty Tricks

Dirty tricks are not about the content. They are ways you can influence emotions when negotiations are going on. Negotiators who are inexperienced are likely to fall for that. When it comes to the content, they prepare very well, but negotiating about something is an emotional process, and having the ability to manipulate emotions can greatly impact the desired result.

Here are some examples:

Trick 1: The anchoring effect

This is when too much weight is given to a counterpart's first offer. If your opponent makes a first offer that is too extreme, you don't deliver a counteroffer immediately. You need to defuse their own offer first before delivering a counteroffer.

Trick 2: The bogey

The negotiator acts as if this point is very important to him or her, but it is not actually very important to him or her. By accepting to let go of this point, the negotiator expects that you concede to something that is also important.

Trick 3: The nibble effect

After you have engaged in long negotiations just before arriving at an agreement, the other individual asks you for a little more, thereby nibbling away at the margin you have set. The reason for this is that the counterpart will accept this in order to prevent the deal from collapsing.

Trick 4: Framing

When you use the right images and words, the desired associations and emotions can be evoked in order to convince the other side. Resistance is usually emotional, unconscious, and irrational.

Numerous dirty tricks exist like the ones we have discussed above that you can use to influence individuals but these tricks are not simply used by top negotiators. On the contrary, they begin with creating the climate that is appropriate, by creating an atmosphere of commitment and willingness. The emotional aspect is where the emphasis is because no cooperative spirit exists at the beginning of the negotiations; the cause is already a lost one.

Understanding Human Behavior to Achieve Successful Negotiations

Negotiation involves understanding and coming to agreements with other individuals. Psychology's insights can effectively bring about an improvement in the results achieved from negotiations since they provide insightful knowledge of human behavior, motives, and decision-making. Psychology plays an important role in negotiations, making it possible for individuals to successfully negotiate deals that both parties find beneficial.

You need to know the following:

Building trust and rapport

When it comes to negotiations, building trust and rapport is important. Psychological concepts like resemblance, reciprocity, and likeability can be used to build a strong interpersonal bond with the other individual.

Promoting collaboration and building trust are made possible through nonverbal communication abilities, empathy, and active listening. By establishing a foundation of trust, negotiators are able to create a setting that is conducive to arriving at solutions that have been mutually agreed to.

Managing conflict and emotions

When discussions are going on, emotions frequently come up and the result may be affected. Emotional intelligence, empathy, and self-regulation are essential traits that assist negotiators when it comes to effective control of their feelings and other people's feelings. Negotiators can prevent the negotiation process from being derailed by disagreements and strive towards achieving settlements that are mutually beneficial by recognizing emotions and resolving them constructively.

Having a full understanding of cognitive biases

Cognitive biases are thought processes that are ingrained and might affect how decisions are made when negotiations are going on. Negotiators are able to modify the approaches they use and the biases are used to their advantage by staying aware of them. Some examples of cognitive biases are the anchoring effect, the endowment effect, and confirmation bias. By being aware of these biases, negotiators can create arguments that are compelling and they can foresee potential challenges in the negotiation process.

Negotiation techniques and strategies

You can gain insights into negotiation tactics and strategies that are successful from psychological studies. Negotiators can come up with plans of action that are successful and accomplish results that are desirable by completely understanding the negotiation power dynamics. These techniques assist negotiators when it comes to building connections that are mutually beneficial and also creating win-win scenarios.

Effective influence and persuasion

Principles of psychological persuasion are crucial in negotiations. You can use scarcity, social evidence, and framing to sway the choice and perception of the other individual. When negotiators can customize their proposals and arguments to appeal to the opposing party's interests, wants, and needs, they have a better chance of achieving results that are favorable.

When you understand the psychology of negotiation, it can help you win more negotiations. A negotiator uses psychology to make the other party perceive what they think. You may not know this, but people are always negotiating.

Psychology is important in negotiation as it plays a major role in the negotiation flow as well as its outcome. Most negotiators pay little attention to using psychology during their negotiations.

You can use the following thoughts to put together psychological components for your negotiations in the future:

Identify the needs of the negotiator

Some negotiators get into a negotiation without thinking about what the other party wants from the negotiation. Such a negotiator puts themselves at a disadvantage. Why is this the case? This is the case because if you have no idea of what the other party wants, you will have no idea of what to offer to make them give you what you desire.

So, if you are still yet to assess the needs of the other negotiator before the negotiation begins, what can you do to accomplish that?

You can ask them to tell you what outcome they desire from the negotiation.

You can also ask them about the outcome that would make both parties win. You can ask a negotiator who has a win-win mindset to understand better.

To ask more subtly, you can ask them what they would like to occur today.

Then, see how far the negotiator will go to get the outcome they stated as the negotiation progresses. Look at what the negotiator is willing to give up to get it. You will be given valuable feedback that will provide you with a sense of your opposition's psychological mindset.

With a win-lose negotiator, they may request concessions that are unreasonable to see what your response will be. So, pay attention and confirm what the other party states as necessary versus what their actions show. A person's actions will always provide you with more insight into the psychology behind why they do the things they do than the words they say.

Identify the individual's emotions and real thoughts through their microexpressions

Microexpressions are unfiltered mental displays of emotion and occur before an individual's mind makes attempts to control the displayed action. The action is real and not contrived when considered from a psychological perspective.

Microexpressions don't last long; they last for about a quarter of a second. Every individual has seven microexpressions that are generic to them. These expressions include disgust, happiness, fear, surprise, sadness, contempt, and anger.

When a person displays disgust, you can use it to validate their internal feelings and gain insight into what is on their mind. The individual who displays disgust will appear to raise their upper lip towards their nose as though a particular thing doesn't smell right.

Through their action, they are letting you know that the offer you have made is not appealing.

Understand that a negotiator may display the same sign of disgust when making an offer to you if they know that the offer is not a good one or they doubt that you will accept it. When this happens, the negotiator may be testing you to see the response you will give to their request.

Read the individual's body language

Body language is important when it comes to negotiations. It is capable of uncovering any hidden clues about what is in your opposition's mind that they did not mention. Thus, the better you are able to interpret the body language of someone, the more insight you will have into the person's thoughts.

When assessing the body gestures of your counterpart, you need to consider the following:

- First, understand how the other negotiator uses their body language in a "normal" situation (whatever their normal is). Then, compare the usage of their normal body language to the changes the negotiator displays when they are stressed, reflective, contemplative, or calm.

For instance, if a negotiation is going on and a negotiator is pleasant throughout the period and makes up and down gestures with their hands, pay attention when the individual's hands turn down and they start to pull gestures towards themselves. The gestures may represent a shift in that individual's mind. Depending on how the negotiation might be influenced by that, you need to take appropriate action to get that individual's mind aligned with your thoughts.

- When a person's arms are crossed, it might mean that they are not receptive or open to an offer or it might not mean that depending on the point you are in the negotiation process.

Some savvy negotiators may feign displeasure by displaying this gesture. The negotiator may do this to either alter the flow of the negotiation or set you up for concession requests that are forthcoming. When you observe this maneuver, you need to be mindful.

To draw the intent out, you need to change the topic of discussion to a topic that your opponent finds favorable. Then, observe what happens to the arms that they crossed. If they still keep their arms crossed, ignore the gesture until they use their words to express their concerns.

A negotiator who emits body language gestures does so based on the triggers of their actions. What triggered their actions can be what was said most recently or it can be an accumulation of the different things.

If you notice that the gestures that are the most recent may cause discomfort in the negotiation, you can ask the other party what their thoughts are. If you believe that the gesture they are displaying is of no importance to the negotiation, you can ignore it.

The important thing is to pay attention to the silent signals you get throughout the negotiation from the body language of an individual. This will help you have an advantage in your negotiations.

When negotiation is going on, psychology can impact the flow of the negotiation. Therefore, a negotiator who is intelligent will alter the other negotiator's mind through the use of many psychological strategies. The better you can use the suggestions discussed above, the better the outcomes of your negotiation will be. And things will be okay. Understand that we are always negotiating.

The use of psychology in negotiations makes understanding the behavior of humans, influencing decisions, controlling emotions, developing rapport, and attaining effective outcomes possible. Negotiators can draw on psychological principles to develop trust, negotiate situations that are challenging, and reach amicable agreements. Individuals who have the ability to attain good outcomes in different circumstances can become great at negotiating by gaining an understanding of the psychological processes that take place in negotiations.

CHAPTER SEVEN
Mindset of a Negotiator

You can win more in sales by using a negotiation mindset. The negotiation tool is strategic and useful in every area of life. Negotiation is important in sales.

Sales use a service or product to solve a customer's problem. However, some sort of pushback often exists from the other side, which can make it hard for the people in sales to reach their goals.

When you use negotiation in your sales strategies, it can make a huge difference in the number of deals you close.

A sales mindset involves convincing a person to buy a service or product from you. This can make other individuals feel that you are a needy person, and it makes them have power over you.

A power imbalance is created and an opportunity is created for them to dictate how you feel, what you say, and what the terms are.

Moving into the mindset of a negotiator is believing you already have a deal. You only need to decide on the product and the terms.

This negotiator mindset equally distributes the power dynamics between the seller and the buyer, and while no individual is more powerful or better than the other individual, as a seller, you can become significantly more persuasive.

When you are at the sales negotiation table, your mindset is what influences your behavior.

Changing into the Mindset of a Negotiator

Practice negotiation actively every day by challenging yourself in daily practice.

You can ask yourself these questions whenever you practice:

- What can you do to receive more than you are expecting to receive?
- What can you do to receive more value from something?

You might ask for an extra thing if you want to try this. For instance, try asking your waitress or waiter to give you a free dessert when you have finished your meal at a restaurant. Understand that the waitress or waiter has the right to say no to you, but even though they say no, that is not the point to look at.

The aim is simply to make you comfortable with being able to ask for more.

When you start practicing these little everyday negotiations, you develop the kind of confidence that is required to close deals that are more substantial.

Confidence on its own is persuasive, and it is key in negotiation. No matter how many skills or negotiation techniques you try to use, people can sense if you don't have confidence. When they sense this, they can gain control over what your response would be.

Avoiding Mistakes in Negotiation

If you want to perfect negotiation, pay attention to when or if you do the following things and then make changes to your approach so you can be more persuasive.

Not wanting to receive a no

It is a normal thing to be afraid to receive a no. However, there is a lot we can learn from being given no as a response. Use the lessons learned from the no you received and ask questions that are open-ended. People will often reject an offer, but if the offer is adjusted to fix the underlying cause of their no or presented in another way, their no turns into a yes. Is this "no" really a true one? Ask yourself if it is a true one or if the no simply means no not yet. If you get to know that it means a no not yet, you should figure out what is making the other party not say yes.

If you have a no-not-yet as the answer, you want to try and find out what is stopping the other individual from saying yes.

Even if you have a true no as the answer, there will always be something you can learn to help you improve yourself for the next opportunity. Consider this an opportunity for you to practice. Learn from the no's that you receive and celebrate the yes's you get.

Not noticing or paying attention to the individual that is in front of you.

It is important to listen to the other party to help you fully understand what the other individual is saying, and also to develop the relationship.

The issue is, most times, we are not really listening to the individual speaking to us. What happens is that we hear the first few words and then we go back internally to think about the response we will give.

When your focus is more on your thoughts, instead of the live conversation, you might miss parts of the conversation that are important. You need to listen actively. This will assist you in understanding better and it will also assist you in understanding where an opportunity may exist to create more value.

Not negotiating, but bargaining

Some buyers and sellers have a practice where they present their desired terms and price and then come to an agreement by meeting somewhere in the middle.

This bargaining is classic. Something you can do is to request for more. You can change the offer's dynamics in your favor by setting your anchor higher. To have a successful outcome of negotiation in sales, you need to stay focused on the right attitude and mindset. Be persistent without being pushy and stay confident that you are going to close the deal that is best for both parties.

Understand that negotiation is an art; so, you need to have persuasive power if you want to make someone take action while avoiding the tactics of manipulation and without making the person feel they are being sold to.

Here is what you can do to maintain a positive mindset during negotiations:

Make adequate preparations

One major factor that is capable of influencing a person's mindset during negotiations is preparation. It can help anticipate possible scenarios, increase confidence, and reduce uncertainty. For proper preparation, define your priorities and goals, such as the things you want to achieve and the reason you want to achieve them, as well as the alternatives you have and walk-away points. Also, do some research on your counterpart to know their priorities and goals, sources of power and leverage, and their weaknesses and strengths. Plan your tactics and strategy for handling questions and objections, communicating your interests and value proposition, and creating and claiming value.

Stay open-minded and flexible

How you adapt and improvise to circumstances that are changing can affect your mindset during negotiations. Negotiations are unpredictable and dynamic, so being open-minded and flexible to adjust your goals, strategies, and priorities is important. Also, your existing skills and resources should be used to solve available problems and create value, as well as to create new options and ideas. Persistence and resilience are needed to get back up from disappointments and failures, while still working towards your interests and goals. Adapting and improvising is capable of helping you deal with uncertainty, handle challenges, and seize opportunities.

Stay focused on the positive aspect.

A great way to boost your creativity, motivation, and mood during negotiations is to remain focused on the positive aspect. To focus on the positive, take time to recognize your achievements and strengths, express appreciation and gratitude, and look for solutions and opportunities. Remind yourself of the things you are proud of and what you are good at, what you appreciate about yourself and are grateful for, how you successfully overcame difficult challenges in the past, the situation, and your counterpart. Check if any opportunities or potential benefits of the negotiation exist that can result in win-win solutions that will keep both parties satisfied.

Communicate and collaborate

How you communicate and collaborate with your counterpart can also influence your mindset during negotiations. Negotiations do not only involve exchanging demands and offers, but also involve building trust, rapport, and understanding. To successfully do this, it is important that you listen attentively and actively to what your counterpart is saying and even what they are not saying, as well as their needs, interests, and concerns. It is important that you ask them questions and clarify any confusion or misunderstandings. Also, sharing perspectives and information can help to build credibility and trust while creating alignment and value. If properly done, communicating and collaborating can help you find common ground, arrive at an agreement that is mutually beneficial, and establish a positive relationship.

Label and properly express your emotions

Another factor that is capable of influencing your mindset when negotiations are going on is how you manage your emotions. Emotions are capable of influencing performance, judgment, and behavior, so managing them properly is important for staying respectful, rational, and calm. To do this, you need to identify your emotions and label them. Be clear about what you are feeling and why you are feeling that way. Once this is done, you should express them. How can you enhance the positive emotions and reduce the negative ones? Also, you need to understand your counterpart's emotions and respond to them. What is your counterpart feeling and why are they feeling that way? Once you have taken these steps, they will assist you in addressing their emotional concerns and needs.

Celebrate yourself

How you learn and grow from the experiences you go through is another factor that is capable of shaping your mindset during negotiations. To make maximum use of your learning and growth, ensure that you ask for input and feedback from your mentors, colleagues, and counterparts. Also, reflecting and evaluating the negotiation is important, considering what you did well and what you could have done better. Ensure that you celebrate and give yourself a reward for any positive results and outcomes of the negotiation that you helped to make happen.

CHAPTER EIGHT
Negotiators and Body Language

Negotiators who are savvy have mastered how to read people's body language and use the information gained to their advantage. However, some negotiators fail to read the nonverbal messages that their counterparts are sending simply because they don't focus and pay attention. Instead, they get so focused on the documents being presented or what is being said and don't look for these vital cues.

People are always negotiating, but they may not know this. Reading body language in this kind of negotiation is just like an intricate dance. But unlike in a dance, when it comes to negotiations, either negotiator will take the lead during the talks. A subtle body language cue will usually show when one individual takes the lead from the other individual.

If you want to improve your body language reading skills, the strategies below will enhance your ability. Once you improve your skills, you will notice other people's gestures. You will have greater insight into their thoughts, giving you an advantage when you are having interactions with them in life and negotiations.

These body language strategies are helpful for negotiators:

Identify the individual's normal behavior

If you want to accurately read the body language of your counterpart, it is important that you first establish that individual's normal behavior or baseline behavior. If you don't do this properly, it is likely that you will misinterpret the person's signals. Baselining involves observing individuals when they are not pressured or stressed. It only takes some minutes to understand how a person behaves in a neutral or relaxed setting, and it is best to do this before the negotiation begins. For example, while you are having coffee and chatting informally. During this time, you can ask a few simple questions that you already know the answers to and observe your counterpart's behavior when they are candid and relaxed.

Do they make eye contact?

Observe if your counterpart's eyes go to one side when providing truthful answers.

Do they smile often?

Which gestures do they display most frequently?

What posture does your counterpart display when they are comfortable?

Once you have understood how your counterpart uses their body in an informal, relaxed context, you will have a baseline that you can use to compare meaningful deviations in body language during the process of negotiation.

Look for gestures appearing in clusters

Nonverbal cues are a group of actions, postures, and movements that reinforce a common point. You can't be trying to decode a person's body language from one single gesture. When gestures appear in clusters or words in sentences, you understand them better. For instance, while an individual's fidgeting may not mean much on its own, if that individual is also pointing his feet toward the door, wringing his hands, and avoiding eye contact, you can be sure that he wants to leave and is feeling distressed. You can look for three body language signals that pass the same nonverbal message.

Observe the individual's engagement, and disengagement signals

During the course of any negotiation stress, engagement, and disengagement are the most important signals to observe in the body language of the other individual. Engagement behaviors such as smiles, head nods, eye contact, forward leans, and so on, indicate agreement, receptivity, or interest. Some gestures can show receptiveness to offers. They make others believe that you are approachable and open-minded. Because displays like these signal moving forward, it is important that you notice when they happen. During those times, you may have those opportunities that are most favorable. Leaning forward, wide eyes, genuine smiles, head up, palms up, open hands, and uncrossed feet, legs, and arms are gestures that indicate receptiveness.

When sensing an individual displaying the signs above, pay attention to how many signs occur at the same time. If some of those actions occur during a specific time, the likelihood that the individual is in a receptive state of mind is heightened.

Disengagement behaviors such as frowns, leaning back, narrowed eyes, looking away, and so on, show that an individual is defensive, angry, or bored.

Look out for stress or discomfort signs

Stress signals such as tightly crossed ankles, face touching, higher vocal tone, and so on, usually accompany discomfort with how the negotiation is turning out or bluffing. When individuals show discomfort signs, it is a sign that they are in distress. When they display the gesture, it will come from a thought they had at that time, which may have come from something that happened earlier in the process of negotiation.

The motion could show their fear of not getting what they want, dislike of the offer you made, or thinking you have caught them in a certain thing they do not want to disclose. When it happens, the point is to raise awareness.

Shifting pace of speech, fidgeting, misquoting what was said, crossing arms, and leaning away are some common signs of discomfort. You need to pay attention to when these signs are displayed. The other individual may use them to confuse you even though the signs may be genuine.

To note how accurate a negotiator's gestures are, you can watch how they use them before the negotiation begins. Then, during your negotiation session, you will have something to compare against.

Observe signs of dejection

When the other individual experiences dejection, points may occur in a negotiation. That may come from the fact that they don't like their position. It could cause adverse effects, such as the individual striking back in ways that are unforeseen to even the playing field. It could also show itself in other forms of irrationality. Slow speech, sadness, lack of energy, hands or arms held close to the body, withdrawal from engagement, and droopy eyes, shoulders, and head are signs to take note of.

Do not dismiss these signs that are being displayed as chance and something you should not bother with. The signals are invaluable and they have the power to influence your negotiations.

Check the context in which the gesture was displayed

A gesture can mean nothing at all or it can be very significant. What matters most is the context in which the individual displays the gesture. Let us use crossed arms as an example: In an audience, most people sitting in the first row will initially cross their arms. They do this because there is no row of chairs in front of them, so they create a barricade with their arms before they lower their guard after warming up to the speaker. In the same way, if your negotiation partner is sitting in a chair without armrests, understand that they might cross their arms as they would when responding to a drop in room temperature.

This is what also makes baselining very important. A person who sits with their arms crossed when thinking or relaxed is sending a message that is different from the message of a person who first displays that gesture immediately after a counteroffer was made by you. This would be meaningful if other signals, such as shoulders that are a little bit positioned away from you and reduced eye contact accompanied the cross arms.

Of course, you won't notice some aspects of the context. A posture that is erect could simply be an indication that the individual has a stiff back or it could be a sign of a tough bargaining position.

It may appear to be a task that is impossible, especially since your conversation will be going on at the same time. What is different now is that you are taking into awareness of this unconscious and innate skill, and you are gaining insight into the thoughts of your counterpart.

Mirror the individual's body language

During negotiation, mirroring takes place when a negotiator imitates the other individual's body language. This is done by negotiators to build trust and rapport. The premise is that by mirroring a person, you appear like that individual. And individuals often like individuals who are like them.

For instance, if the other individual sits upright, you can sit upright. If the individual starts talking at a particular pace, you can speak at the same pace. This is also the case for hand gestures. You can use your hands to make slow gestures if they use their hands to gesture slowly.

You can establish rapport and build trust faster by using mirroring, which can make you win negotiations faster. Just be careful so that your actions do not appear as mockery. That could cause issues in trust and rapport.

Observe facial expressions and eye contact

Eye contact is meaningful when it occurs and even when it doesn't. An individual expresses interest in what has happened or in the discussion when their eyes widen. A person's eyes are pin-pointedly focused when they narrow. And that gesture can show excitement with the negotiation's occurrence or it can indicate displeasure. You can study other facial expressions to understand what they mean.

Facial expressions are capable of uncovering hidden and real emotions in negotiations. That is why interpreting these expressions and other body language gestures accurately will give you a huge advantage during the interactions you have with others.

Uncovering deception

Negotiators use different forms of deception during negotiations. This may be done by not revealing the whole truth and using misdirection to avoid stating their position, as well as in other ways. Negotiators can deceive you with some outright lie.

Observe the following if you notice that an individual may be trying to deceive you:

The individual is maintaining too much eye contact because they do not want you to think that they are deceiving you or the individual is avoiding eye contact.

The individual is covering their mouth with their hands when they speak.

The individual is smiling inappropriately when there is no reason for it.

The individual is rubbing their legs, arms, and neck.

Forcing gestures such as arms crossed while sneering, finger pointing, and fist banging.

Access the intent and observe the point of origin when you see any of these gestures. The individual may be trying to derail your effort to continue their deception.

You will win more negotiations when you are able to read body language. When you witness eye contact, use mirroring, notice facial expressions, analyze body posture, scrutinize hand gestures, and perceive speaking speed, you will gain insights into the emotions, thoughts, and intentions of other individuals. And all will be okay with the world. Don't forget that you are always negotiating.

Using Body Language to Improve Negotiation

Not sure where to look or what to do with your hands? Your habit of close-talking or crossing your legs could be working in the opposite direction to your words.

You will find strong negotiation skills advantageous throughout your life. These negotiation skills rest largely on your ability to back up the words you say with physical actions that show confidence, honesty, and openness. This increases the other individual's desire to cooperate and reach an agreement. It also builds trust.

Studies show that non-verbal communication and body language impact a discussion more than the words you say.

A large number of messages are conveyed to people through nonverbal cues like posture and gestures, and research has shown that body language accurately gauges an individual's true intentions and attitudes more than their words or tone of voice. According to research, a large percentage of people are more likely to retain information that was passed to them both visually and orally.

Use body language and non-verbal tips to increase your success rate in negotiations and remain ahead of the game. You have a high likelihood of winning negotiations if you do this right.

You can improve your negotiations by doing the following:

Arrive on time

A large percentage of success means showing up. You make a first impression on a potential boss or new client before you even meet them or say a word.

The negotiation process is damaged by lateness in two ways: It is seen as discourteous and shows incompetence as well as a lack of integrity on the latecomer's part, thereby irritating the other individual and making them less likely to accept an agreement. Also, the anxiety that you will have when you arrive late will destroy the confident, focused, and calm demeanor that you will need if you are to achieve success in the negotiation. So, ensure that you show up on time and give yourself a chance to achieve your goal.

Master the handshake

After arriving on time, the next thing is the handshake which is often dreaded. A handshake is enough for some people to seal deals. The perfect handshake has sealed many deals over the years. Studies show that a handshake promotes honesty, makes individuals feel comfortable, and increases the cooperative behaviors that result in deal-making.

Have negotiations with the right individuals

Since a large part of your ability to set a positive tone to negotiate successfully rests on the way you control your body language, your intuition in responding to the non-verbal cues and body language of your potential opponents before deciding to have any engagement with them does this as well. When a decision is made to sit down, the game's outcome is often more than half decided.

Maintain space

Proxemics, which is the science of personal space, focuses on the distance that exists between individuals as they interact. Have you ever felt incredibly pressured or uncomfortable when a colleague at work, an acquaintance, or a stranger stood a little too close to you while they were speaking with you? Did you find yourself no longer paying attention to what they were saying and were shuffling your feet and silently wishing the individual moved further away?

The negotiation process can be completely disrupted by such a situation. It is important for each individual to feel that they are not being physically intimidated and that their personal space is being respected. One rule that is safe is to stand or sit at least four feet away and observe the other individual to study their comfort level.

Maintain positive facial expressions

You must not be a business tycoon to know the often unwelcome effects that your facial expressions can have on a discussion's outcome. Any individual who has ever been in a relationship with someone has probably experienced the outcome of their unintentional facial expressions when they are in the middle of a conversation and their partner stops and asks them what their look means.

Whether you like it or not, your facial expressions can affect a negotiation's outcome, so do your best to make sure that your facial expressions enhance your positive verbal cues. Avoid frowning your forehead like someone who is worried and take time to smile. You can also nod to agree with what they are saying. Keep your eyes level and your chin up to evoke positivity. The other individual will be looking at you to see that your physical gestures mirror the words you say. So, keep your physical gestures and words positive and open.

Maintain consistent and friendly eye contact

Eye contact is a powerful tool of communication as it conveys trust, sincerity, and openness. When you avoid eye contact during a negotiation, it prevents you from building a good rapport. The other individual feels like you are being dishonest or evasive, and this can make the negotiation hard.

Eye contact is powerful and when it is done too much, it can be seen as intimidating or aggressive as too much of it is threatening. Ensure that you maintain consistent eye contact, but understand that you can also look away when processing or thinking. Doing this is natural.

Keep your hands away from your face

Our hands are highly expressive and are capable of adding a lot to the communication we have. When negotiating, it is recommended that your hands be kept away from your face. Rubbing your head or face is generally considered a symptom of anxiety, and you don't want to appear anxious during a negotiation.

Similarly, keeping your hands over your eyes or mouth shows that you may be trying to lie or hide something. Appear truthful and confident by keeping your hands open, unclenched, and away from your face as much as you can.

Keep your legs and arms uncrossed

Your body should exude calm, confidence, and strength in the same way that you want your words to exude calm, confidence, and strength during a negotiation. If you are a person who is always tapping your feet or fingers, crossing and uncrossing your legs, or entwining your hands, it will convey the message that you are in a stressed state and not a relaxed state. Ensure that you limit the movement of your hands to expression rather than fidgeting and also keep your legs calm.

Non-verbal channels are more powerful for communicating feelings and interpersonal attitudes than the verbal channel.

Similarly, any level of crossed hands or limbs will be interpreted as closed off or negative, which won't assist you in creating trust in any negotiation. No individual wants to talk to a person who appears to already have their mind made up. So, get your legs and arms uncrossed and maintain some distance between your hands to appear ready to listen to the points of view of the other individual and to stay open-minded.

Reduce your speed and keep quiet

Every individual, no matter the situation they find themselves in, wants to feel heard, considered, and respected before a counter-move is made. However, the negotiation's stress, combined with your desire to get your point across and your excitement, can make you overenthusiastic to the point of talking over the other individual or even rushing your words. Listen carefully to the other individual, pause a little to show them that you are giving what they said a thought, and ensure that you keep your response calm and slow. This shows confidence and respect in your position.

Individuals remember about twenty percent of the information that is given to them visually and about ten percent of the information that is provided to them orally. However, an individual retains about eighty percent of the information that is presented to them both visually and orally, meaning that body language and being vocal are equally important.

Learn to be silent sometimes. You may be surprised by the effects. Never forget that there is power in silence. Pausing for a while can give you time to think before getting back to your negotiation. It can also make your opponent get back in line.

CHAPTER NINE
Dealing with Emotions in Negotiations

Emotions are important in negotiation. Most individuals focus on local arguments, facts, and figures when it comes to negotiations. However, emotions are a key piece of the puzzle that people often overlook. Negotiations are capable of being emotionally charged, and when these feelings are ignored, it can result in mistrust, resistance, and a communication breakdown. Emotions matter when negotiation is involved, and acknowledging your emotions can result in better outcomes. You need to learn how to manage your emotions and use them to your advantage.

Negotiations do not only occur when you exchange information and make offers. They also involve understanding the needs and motivations of the other individual, forming relationships, and looking for common ground. Emotions are an important part of this whole process. When you acknowledge the other individual's emotions and address them, you show them that you care about their views and are also willing to work together with them to arrive at a solution that is mutually beneficial. When this happens, it can start a positive feedback loop where both individuals become more cooperative and open.

Sympathy and empathy are different things, even though they are often used interchangeably. Empathy is a person's ability to step into the shoes of another individual, to understand their views and feelings, and to guide actions through the use of that understanding. It involves feeling with an individual. On the other hand, sympathy involves feeling for someone. It is feeling compassion for another individual's misfortune, and it is a more detached and distant response.

In the negotiation world, empathy is more effective than sympathy, and the reason is that empathy helps you to have a complete understanding of your counterpart's desires, needs, and motivations, giving you the upper hand when it comes to creating solutions that satisfy both individuals. It promotes trust and encourages a deeper connection, building a strong foundation for a successful negotiation. Although sympathy may be well-intentioned, it can result in condescension or pity, thereby undermining the process of negotiation and giving too much away.

One thing is to acknowledge emotions, but managing your response to emotions is another thing. Both individuals may feel a range of emotions when a negotiation is going on, including frustration, anger, excitement, and anxiety. As a negotiator, you need to pay attention to your emotions and how they are capable of influencing your behavior and decisions. It is also important that you recognize and validate the other individual's emotions, even if they don't have the same perspective as you and you disagree with their perspective. You may not be able to control how you feel, but what you do as a result of that feeling is something you can control. This can assist with building trust and diffusing negativity.

It will be hard for people to read you if you show no emotion. This could be beneficial. But there is also a downside to this. By showing emotions that are planned, the other individual can be conditioned to feel what you feel. Whether it be disgust or happiness, showing planned emotions is capable of making your message land better. Of course, using emotions authentically and strategically is important, rather than using emotions as a manipulative tool.

Here are some tips to help you achieve success in navigating emotionally charged negotiations:

- Make sure that you are actively listening to the emotions and words of the other individual and that you are fully present.

- Respond to the emotions of the other individual with understanding and empathy. Acknowledge their perspective even if you don't agree with it.
- Focus on the fundamental needs and interests of both individuals instead of getting bogged down in fixed positions.
- Although emotions may run high, you need to remain calm and centered. Stay focused on the goal of finding a solution that is mutually beneficial and stay focused on the facts.
- Remain open to new solutions and ideas, even if they are not the same as your initial expectations. Don't forget that the process of negotiation is a collaborative one.

Negotiations can be challenging and complex, but you can create more productive and positive outcomes by acknowledging emotions. You can build rapport and trust by validating the emotions of both individuals. Strategically using emotions is capable of helping you to arrive at win-win agreements. These tips will help you to be better prepared to navigate emotionally charged negotiations and accomplish the goals you have.

One topic that is guaranteed to raise emotions is negotiation. For many individuals, just thinking about a negotiation that is coming up can increase anxiety, and the actual negotiation can make you feel worse. You have a personal interest in the negotiation's outcome, and the stakes are usually high.

Emotions are capable of becoming too extreme sometimes, and this is not surprising. You cannot express emotions in an extreme way. This behavior would produce a negative effect in any negotiation.

So, how can you get the best deal with emotions in negotiations?

Let us take a look at the emotions we have leading up to a negotiation, the ones we have during a negotiation, the emotions we have in a negotiation, and the emotions after a negotiation.

Your emotions at the beginning of a negotiation

How we feel at the beginning of a negotiation when we sit down at the table to negotiate, is one way in which negotiations are impacted by emotions.

When individuals experience anxiety in negotiating, it is usually caused by unpredictability, a lack of control, and an absence of feedback on the performance of the negotiator.

You can reduce the feelings of unpredictability and lack of control with planning and good preparation. You will appear more powerful and confident if you prepare well, and you will be more in control.

When you plan and consider everything that the other individual is likely to bring up in the negotiation, you will know how to respond to them and the trades you can make, unpredictability is reduced, and you will be less likely to be thrown by whatever they come up with.

You will be more powerful if you feel more powerful as power is in the head. Good planning and preparation have a lot to do with this. Posture may also have a lot to do with this.

Research has shown that some specific postures directly influence our hormone balance. Individuals who adopt power poses have a decrease in the stress hormone, cortisol, and an increase in the dominance hormone, testosterone. Power poses involve sitting upright and taking up as much body space as possible. Individuals using submissive postures don't experience this but the opposite. This means that we could feel less powerful or more powerful depending on how we sit in a negotiation.

Your emotions during the negotiation

Skilled negotiators do not have nerves of steel. They also talk about their emotions. This behavior is effective. Our emotions reveal something personal about us which can make the other side trust us. Arguing with another individual's emotions is hard. If you say you are concerned that you won't be able to meet a deadline, it is impossible for the other individual to say, no you are not concerned.

Understand that this behavior is simply a commentary on your emotions and internal thoughts meaning that you stay in control of your own emotions. This does not mean weeping, throwing a tantrum, or threatening the other individual with a firearm.

A lack of feedback also causes anxiety about negotiations. The negotiator will always have feedback as a problem. They may get a well done for getting the deal, but not receive any constructive feedback on the things they actually did during the negotiation.

Negotiators need to receive feedback in such a way that they can identify specific areas to work on when the next negotiation comes. Even negotiators who are highly experienced discover that they can tweak their own behavior when they get such feedback.

The emotions of other individuals during a negotiation

We have talked about our own emotions. What about the emotions of other individuals during a negotiation? Intense series of attacks or defensive behaviors may happen between two or more people. It becomes personal when there is a shift of focus from the problem to the individual.

Not surprisingly, research has shown that negotiators who are skilled should avoid getting themselves involved in defend-and-attack spirals. You need to withdraw from the negotiation when it gets to this point. You may find it difficult in the heat of the moment to avoid getting involved in a defend-and-attack spiral, but you must do your best to withdraw from the negotiation when you find yourself at this point.

You can easily substitute another behavior that is more useful, rather than trying to avoid a behavior that may cause issues. So, when you find yourself facing an attack, instead of attacking back, do your best to get to the source of the attack and understand the reason behind it. Once you have established the cause of the attack, you can start working together for a solution to the problem. If you notice that the emotional temperature is still too high, what you can do is ask for a break and then return when things have cooled a little.

Your emotions at the end of a negotiation

After the event, ensure that you properly review the negotiation. This can be done by having a quiet reflection about what happened when you are in a car driving back to the office. Do a full review of the outcomes against your plan, making sure that you look at the areas that went well and the areas that need improvement so that you know exactly what to do when the time for the next negotiation comes.

There might be a need for you to watch some television, listen to calming music, or take a walk, but, whatever you do, don't hold a grudge against your counterpart.

Negotiating is an activity that humans engage in and emotions make us human. No matter how much we try, we cannot remove emotions from negotiation. We can only acknowledge them, both in other individuals and in ourselves, and manage them appropriately.

Negotiating Effectively with Emotional Intelligence

One thing that great negotiators know how to do is that they know how to make other individuals give them what they want. What are the things that make a great negotiator great at negotiating? What things make the average negotiator average? Are skills the only thing involved? Are strategies all that is involved? Is it only emotional intelligence that is involved?

The ability to negotiate can be learned and then honed with continuous practice. It is a skill. Negotiation doesn't mean you have to hurt others to make yourself happy. You are trying to get what you want when you go into a negotiation. The other individual is also trying to get what they want. Both of you can get what you want when you first understand what you want. Most individuals think that negotiation is when you win or lose, but creating value is what negotiation is really about. If you don't first have a complete understanding of what the other individual wants, you can't create value. This is where skills come in. You need to be skilled in what you are negotiating about.

You also need to figure out what you are willing to give up if you want to get that thing that you want. This is not about being mean or being nice. It involves figuring out what you can do to get what you want. To achieve that, you will have to do a counterintuitive thing. You will have to give up what you want. This is where the need to have strategies comes in. You need to plan your strategies ahead of time before you start the negotiation.

The ability to manage emotions is required to implement strategies. Emotions also play a key role in our negotiations since they play a key role in our lives.

Emotional Intelligence, also referred to as EQ, is a concept that has become more popular in recent times, especially when negotiations are involved. Schools don't usually teach emotional intelligence, and it is not something that can be automatically learned overnight. But it can definitely be improved over time. High EQ is usually associated with successful negotiation, as it assists you in understanding the individual you are having negotiations with better. The average individual only has a twenty-five percent chance of achieving their goals for a negotiation. With EQ, your chances can be increased to at least seventy-five percent. So, how can you define emotional intelligence?

Emotional Intelligence, also known as EQ, is an individual's ability to identify their own emotions and manage them as well as the emotions of other individuals. What is important here is the emotions of other individuals.

If you have ever met an individual who is capable of having effective communication even in stressful situations, turning a bad mood into a good mood, or changing a bad situation into a good situation, you have met an individual who has a high level of emotional intelligence. Individuals with high emotional intelligence possess many skills that make them great when it comes to negotiating, communicating, and leading.

Academics have developed various models of EQ. They include models by John Mayer, Peter Salovey, David Caruso, and David Goleman. Four branches of emotional intelligence are described by Mayer and Salovey's model. Perceiving emotions, which is the first branch, is an individual's ability to accurately perceive emotions in themselves and in other individuals. Using emotions, which is the second branch, is an individual's ability to access and generate emotions that create thought. Understanding emotions, which is the third branch, is a person's ability to understand emotions, as well as to understand the information provided by emotions. Managing emotions, which is the fourth branch, is a person's ability to regulate emotions, including enhancing the emotions if appropriate and changing them if necessary. Mayer and Salovey also talked about two higher-order abilities, which include emotional management and emotional self-awareness.

Emotional Intelligence, which we have said is also known as EQ, is about the self-control and self-awareness that an individual has. An individual who has high emotional intelligence can use this during negotiating as it will assist them in making a decision in a non-stressful manner, and they will not become too stressed.

An emotionally intelligent negotiator needs to have the following skills:

They need to possess the ability to control their emotions.

They need to possess the ability to read the emotions of their opponent and also anticipate their opponent's response to certain situations.

Every one of us are emotional beings. Our emotions are important when it comes to effective communication. However, a clear difference exists between empathy and emotional intelligence (EQ).

Empathy is often associated with Emotional Intelligence (EQ) by most individuals, and it is a very important skill. Empathy is a person's ability to view things from the perspective of the other individual, and this skill is important when negotiations are involved. You are emotionally intelligent if you have the ability to recognize and manage your own emotions and those of other individuals.

Understand that showing empathy during a negotiation does not mean that you are a weak person. If the other individual takes it as a sign of weakness, then you need to reset the negotiation's tone.

CHAPTER TEN
Attitude in Negotiation

Our disposition is what makes us happy, not our position. Remember, while some people ski in the winter, others freeze. Positive results always come from a positive attitude. A positive attitude may seem like something little, but it makes a huge difference in our lives. Successful negotiation needs positive energy as well as the creation of an environment that promotes cooperation. The energy you diffuse and the attitude with which you enter a negotiation play a key role in the success of that negotiation. Positive energy raises your confidence level and your stress-absorbing capacity. It opens your mind and makes you more influential. If you adopt a positive attitude, individuals will also be friendlier.

When a negotiator's mind is positively charged, they will make fewer mistakes, and they will also feel empowered. Negativity narrows an individual's focus and makes them focus wrongly on themselves.

Before you start negotiating, your mind and body should be brought into a positive state. Ensure that you maintain this state to the highest possible extent throughout the duration of the negotiation. There are many factors that can keep you from getting to this optimum state. They include your distractions, physiology, what you ate before the meeting, the setting in which the negotiation takes place, and so on. Make sure that you stay in control of these factors before you start negotiating.

Resetting your physiology is one great way in which you can trigger positivity. Check the posture you have, open your chest, and ensure that your breathing is calm and deep. Practice a sense of presence and wear a smile on your face. Do not start a conference call or enter meetings sighing, squinting, or slouching. Your body greatly influences your mind; scientists refer to this as embodied cognition. Your physical state is capable of generating a negative or positive response in your mind. Smiling and laughing, for instance, trigger positive emotions.

You are also feeding your mind with the right data when your attitude is right. If you allow everything to enter your mind and you don't pay attention, negative thoughts from others and yourself will affect you and it will spread. It will impact your energy level as well as your performance. You need to guard your mind and prevent negativities from getting in and taking over your life.

The human mind is naturally built to respond to information that is negative. We don't pay attention to good news the way we pay attention to bad news, and negativity plays a key role as far as the decision-making process is concerned. Avoid exposing yourself too much to negative people and negative news. Practice relaxation and meditation to reduce negative thoughts.

A Positive Attitude and Contract Negotiation

A mindset that focuses on the benefits, opportunities, and solutions that come from any situation, and not focusing on the obstacles, drawbacks, and difficulties, is a positive attitude. A positive attitude is not when you deny the reality of the challenges you are experiencing and it does not mean ignoring the challenges, but rather acknowledging them and coming up with ways to overcome them. A person with a positive attitude is confident, optimistic, and resilient, and they also express appreciation, gratitude, and respect for themselves and other individuals.

You have a positive attitude when you are able to listen to others and put yourself in their shoes. Ask questions about why you need this, why it is important, or why you want to give up on this. Negotiating can be likened to a two-way street, to be successful you need an open and positive attitude. Ensure that your negotiations are enriched with different perspectives, have a positive attitude, and stay open toward other disciplines that contribute. This will help you achieve greater things together.

A positive attitude will give a person room to display creativity, offering solutions to a contract negotiation that is a win-win negotiation. Contract negotiations have to do with arriving at an agreement that will benefit both individuals. It is easy sometimes and difficult at other times. Negotiations require effort and time and you may experience disappointments sometimes that you can learn from and apply the lessons to future negotiations. You will make friends, and as the challenge gets harder, your relationship gets deeper.

It is important to bring a positive attitude to the negotiations. This will help you to share compelling insights that will rightly direct the conversation. A more favorable context will ultimately be shown by the outcome of the negotiation when working with a positive approach to provide value and find the need. Working in this way to come up with a win-win gives the parties involved a feeling of partnership. The scene for the next negotiation and discussion is always being set by you.

A positive attitude is necessary for the negotiation of contracts. When you have a positive attitude during the negotiation of a contract, it is capable of significantly impacting your performance and results. Your energy and motivation can be boosted, thereby enhancing your problem-solving skills and creativity. Your rapport and communication with your counterpart are also improved, helping you build goodwill and trust. A positive attitude is capable of increasing your happiness with the process as well as the outcome, and it can also increase your satisfaction. It can keep you enthusiastic, engaged, and focused, even when you are experiencing disagreements or setbacks. It helps you to generate more alternatives, options, and ideas for achieving your goals, while also satisfying both parties' needs. It also reduces negative emotions that may cause damage to the relationship and helps you manage conflicts constructively. Ultimately, it makes it possible for you to learn from the mistakes you have made, celebrate your achievements, and appreciate the contract's value for your organization and yourself.

Sometimes both individuals involved in a negotiation hit a specific issue or clause that generates negative goodwill on both sides. When you remain positive in both statements and views, it is still possible for you to make progress and then later get back to the problematic situation. Both parties have made good progress. At that point, the other party might decide to soften their initial stance to get the deal done.

You can approach a contract negotiation in two main ways. It is an opportunity and it is a fight. Having an attitude that is positive leads to great outcomes. Take the points of contention as opportunities to learn even if there are points of contention. There is a lot you can learn about your competitors, market environment, and even your customers by the points that are raised. There will be times when the other individual is negative, aggressive, or determined to have their way and you will find these interactions more challenging. Beginning with an open mind and a positive attitude will assist you in achieving a positive outcome and forming a relationship that is good with your customer.

So, how can a positive attitude be developed for contract negotiation?

You can learn how to develop a positive attitude for the negotiation of contracts, practice, and improve the attitude over time. Preparation is important, as it assists you when it comes to clarifying your interests and goals, as well as understanding your counterpart's interests and goals. Setting positive and realistic expectations for the negotiation is also important, rather than thinking that it will be hostile or difficult. Positive affirmations are capable of helping you reinforce your beliefs and positive attitude. You can repeat statements like, "I am grateful for this negotiating opportunity" or "I am a capable and competent negotiator." Also, adopting body language that is positive can help you convey openness and confidence. Seeking feedback from others and learning from your past experience can help you identify the weaknesses and strengths that you have. You will solve problems more effectively, communicate more effectively, achieve better outcomes, and feel happier and more satisfied when you use a positive attitude for contract negotiation.

Negotiation and a Problem-Solving Attitude

When negotiations are going on and things become uncomfortable, we may want to keep holding on to our position. Although this may be appropriate at times, you need to ensure that you do it in a way that is consistent with the values of your organization and in a professional way. A problem-solving attitude is capable of helping you.

When we talk about a problem-solving attitude, it means that you should be open-minded. It does not mean that you should instantly compromise or give in every time you don't agree with the views of the client. In other words, you keep letting them know that you are willing and open to hearing about different ways in which you can approach the situation and arrive at a solution that is mutually acceptable.

You can show open-mindedness through the use of this approach where you paraphrase what was said and look for value in the suggestion that was made.

Also, you need to remember to acknowledge the objections of the client before beginning to negotiate. Let the client know that you heard what they said and look for something positive that you can say about the client's point of view. Then give an honest response.

Let the client know that you completely understand their position and that you can see how valuable what they have said is.

So, for instance, if a client desires to make changes to the terms associated with a recommendation, you can tell them that you understand why they would like to make changes to the terms, but you would like to explain how the particular changes they want to make would be difficult for your organization.

When you are negotiating, remember that you have a goal, just like the client does. Don't criticize them or do anything that will embarrass them. Let them know that you are striving to reach a solution that is mutually acceptable. You need to understand that you can achieve this with a problem-solving mindset. This problem-solving mindset will help you close more deals and accomplish greater things in the future.

CONCLUSION

Negotiation is an important aspect of human interaction that takes place in various contexts, from diplomacy and business deals to personal relationships and everyday conversations. It involves finding solutions that are mutually acceptable between parties with differing needs, interests, and perspectives. To successfully navigate negotiation's complex landscape, it is essential to grasp common negotiation principles and apply them. These negotiation principles provide a framework for effective collaboration, conflict resolution, and communication. You need to understand negotiation rules, and this is crucial.

Empathy, clear communication, and active listening are emphasized by negotiation principles. By understanding these principles, you can communicate your priorities, concerns, and interests more effectively, creating an environment that is conducive to productive discussions.

You need to have a clear understanding of what you want to achieve before you get into any negotiation. It is important that you know what your alternatives are and the least you are willing to accept from the negotiation. Having this knowledge will help you have expectations that are realistic and you will be able to prioritize your interests and not allow yourself to get sidetracked by unimportant issues. Researching the other party's constraints, needs, and goals will make it easy for you to understand their perspective. It will also be easy for you to find common ground.

Understand that effective communication is important. You need to be able to communicate clearly as clear communication is important in any negotiation. Communication is important for the negotiation of contracts without confrontation, as it assists you in clarifying your expectations, conveying your message, and resolving any disputes or misunderstandings. You should communicate confidently, clearly, and concisely, using language that is simple and precise, avoiding technical or jargon terms, and confirming that you understand everything. You should also communicate assertively, politely, and respectfully, using a positive and calm tone, avoiding distractions or interruptions, and addressing any concerns or issues.

Confidence is important in any negotiation. And during negotiation, a negotiator can convey their message through body language. To convey your message, you can make eye contact, stand up straight, and use expansive and open gestures to show that you are sure of your position and yourself. Avoid fidgeting or crossing your arms when possible. It can show a lack of discomfort, insecurity, or credibility.

Remember to enhance your likeability through mirroring. Mirroring has to do with consciously mimicking the movement and body language of the individual with whom you are interacting. This can build rapport and make the other individual feel more receptive to your offers, counteroffers, and ideas, and also feel more comfortable. Doing this too much can make you appear manipulative or insincere, dampening your ability to make deeper connections, so be sure to use mirroring subtly.

When you are negotiating, being able to read body language and interpret it accurately can give you a huge advantage. The ability to read an individual's body language will help you detect some things that may not be conveyed by the spoken word. The body language reading skill can be applied in various contexts in which the ability to persuade, negotiate, or simply learn by understanding the point of view of the other individual is important. Accurately reading body language during any of your endeavors or during negotiations, will help you when it comes to earning you money, interacting more efficiently with people, and enhancing every area of your life.

Don't forget that win-win strategies make it possible for multiple parties to find solutions that are mutually beneficial while conducting negotiations. This approach is capable of helping you avoid conflict between negotiators and it also provides benefits to everyone involved in the negotiation. If frequent negotiations with external parties are included in your job, you might find it beneficial to gain more knowledge about win-win strategies.

All parties benefit from the final contract or agreement in a win-win situation. An individual who is using a win-win strategy seeks to provide benefits to all the parties that are part of a negotiation. Understand that collaboration is important in this strategy.

You need to listen more and talk less. This rule of negotiation is important as it can make or break your outcome goals. The more you know about the other individual, the better off you are, and the less they know about you, the stronger your position. When you listen actively, it helps you gather information about the thought processes, concerns, and goals of the other individual. You maintain more control over the negotiation dynamics when you reveal less about your own position.

You can also get outside assistance if necessary. You can get a third party that will help you come up with a win-win solution. They can help both sides of the negotiation come up with innovative solutions and concessions that benefit everybody. A third party can also make suggestions about options and proposals that have not been previously considered by the parties that are originally negotiating. Third parties also make it possible for both parties involved in a negotiation to share information that is sensitive, providing fairness and trust to negotiations that are challenging. Choosing an outside negotiator who is a neutral person to each of the individuals involved in the negotiation is important to reduce the chance of errors and individual gains.

Do your best to find a deal that is good for both parties and work towards a win-win situation. Ensure that you embrace the concept of a win-win resolution to create more positive and sustainable outcomes. Look for solutions that all parties involved in the negotiation will find beneficial rather than seeing negotiations as battles. When you are a winner, it means that you don't see negotiations as a battle and you embrace the concept of win-win negotiations.

When you follow the guidelines we have given in this book, you can enhance your negotiation skills and achieve better outcomes. You will find all that we have discussed in this book helpful in your personal and professional life. Your conflict resolution techniques will be refined and you will achieve better results when you incorporate these strategies into your approach. You will become a better negotiator and understand what is on people's minds before you even make your offer or present your proposal to them.

Printed in Great Britain
by Amazon